# Legacy of faith and love

## The life story of Norma Martinez

**Ruth Arias**

First paperback edition January 2022

Book design by Aeysha Mahmood
Book Translation by Ruth Arias & Abril Rodriguez
Book editing by Amanda Carrion & Renee Rawe

ISBN 979-8-9853230-0-9 (Paperback)

Books By Love
18331 Pines Blvd
Unit #133
Pembroke Pines, FL 33029

More books available at:

www.booksbylove.com

booksbylove.com

*For my grandmother Norma:*
*You always said your life was a book.*
*Here's your book!*
*I love you with all my heart and miss you dearly.*
*With love,*
*your granddaughter and friend*
*Ruth (Rusa)*

# Table of contents

Chapter 1

# A Glorious Morning

It was a beautiful morning. A very special Friday, on January 11, 2019. The sun was bright and warm, the soft and melodious wind moved the palm trees back and forth. Through the window the sound of little birds singing brighten the morning. As I was getting my daughter Sophia ready for school, it felt as if I could smell a sweet fragrance of peace filling my house. All I could think of at that very moment was about my beautiful grandmother, Abuelita Norma. I prayed that God would take her home so that she would no longer suffer. I thanked Him for the gift of her long life, which was a great blessing to all who knew her. I was sure that when that moment came, she would be surrounded by her children and loved ones, as was her greatest desire. My heart longed to be with her in the last moments of her life. My grandma was not only a mother, grandmother and great-grandmother; she was the most special and influential person to our family and to many who had the privilege of knowing her. This extraordinary woman was the most wonderful person I had ever met in my entire life. Norma Rodriguez Evangelista de Martinez, was her name.

On that glorious morning, at 86 years of age, Norma Martinez was reunited with the beloved of her heart, Jesus Christ. It was a cloudy and cold morning in Queens, New York and my grandmother was at her daughter's house, Maria (better known as Maribel). There, surrounded by her daughters and after days without opening her eyes, she opened them for the very last time. God gave her the opportunity to open them for the last time to say goodbye to her family with a peaceful look. Her gaze was very deep and penetrating. With a beautiful smile she looked at my aunts and her home attendant. Although she didn't say a word, her gaze filled with love said it all. Everyone there drew closer to her with tear-filled eyes and holding her hand they gazed at each other for a few minutes before she closed her eyes again, taking her last breath. In that moment, the angels came for her soul and a swift wind was felt blowing throughout the room. My aunts who were there by her side could literally feel the departure of her soul as time seemed to stand still. One of Norma's greatest wishes was to die surrounded by her children at home. She didn't want to pass away in a hospital, but at home with her family in complete peace. All of her family and the people who dearly loved her were able to be by her side during the last weeks of her life. Those were precious moments full of love with her family, just as she had longed for.

Abuelita's breast cancer started in her left breast and in the course of only two years, shortly after a partial mastectomy, the cancerous cells spread rapidly throughout her body and metastasized. Norma did not want to expose herself to further treatments because in her heart she already felt it was the end of her journey. I remember, almost two months prior to her departure, the moment when the doctors came into the room to give us the terrible news of what they had seen in the x-ray tests. Abuelita had been feeling very weak with severe bone pain for weeks. She was in very poor health and her general practitioner could not give her a diagnosis that clearly explained what she was feeling in her body. We decided to take her to the emergency room for further tests. There that afternoon it was just she and I when the doctors came into the room and asked me to sit down to give me the news. I looked at my Abuelita with teary eyes, not even wanting to think of the news I was about to hear. Her eyes were fixed on mine as if she was transferring peace to me. I sat down and took a deep breath. I held her hand so she could feel my support and began to listen to what the doctors had found in her body. As I listened to them speak, I felt as if a bucket of ice water had been thrown on me. I was frozen, totally horrified. I couldn't believe what I was hearing.

"Ruth, are you okay? There is not much we can do for your grandmother anymore. The cancer is too advanced. We are very sorry." The doctors left the room and I couldn't, truly, couldn't hold back my tears. I began to cry inconsolably with my grandmother there beside me. At that moment I couldn't even look at her. I couldn't cry out to God; nothing came out of me but a deep cry from my soul. I didn't want to believe what I was hearing. I was devastated and confused. But in the midst of the pain, my beautiful Abuelita held me, she took me by the hand and gave me a tight hug. I collapsed into her arms, as I always did, because I felt safe there. Wiping away my tears, I could feel in her arms an inexplicable peace filling my body and heart. "Rusa..." she said to me, in her sweet and tender voice, "Daughter, my life is in the best hands; in the hands of my Jesus."

Throughout my life, like my grandmother, I have always been a woman of great faith. My mother (eldest daughter Hilcia) and my grandmother instructed us in that great faith, and we knew the God of the impossible. At the moment when I heard this news, my faith was radically tested, I could not believe that my grandmother, the strongest woman I had ever known, the pillar of faith in our family, the woman who was so special to God and to all of us, was going through this.

That glorious day, January 11, 2019, at about 9:10 in the morning, I got a call from my Aunt Ruth. Seeing her name on my cell phone made my heart skip a beat. I picked up the call and heard my aunt's crying voice saying, "Rusa, mom just parted with the Lord." She took a deep breath and began to cry inconsolably. In that instant I could see a movie in my head of all the beautiful moments I had lived with my Abuelita. She was an inspiring woman in every aspect. I could see the moments as a child when I would fall asleep in her arms. I could see the happy moments when she would give us the best advice while cooking for the whole family. I saw her smile and heard her voice that always prayed and blessed us so that Psalm 1 would be fulfilled in us. Grandma did everything with so much love. And, that love marked her whole family, as it will also mark the generations to come, forever.

This beautiful Psalm says,

*Blessed is the one*
*who does not walk in step with the wicked*
*or stand in the way that sinners take*
*or sit in the company of mockers,*

*but whose delight is in the law of the* LORD,
*and who meditates on his law day and night.*
*That person is like a tree planted by streams of water,*
*which yields its fruit in season*
*and whose leaf does not wither—*
*whatever they do prospers.*
*Psalm 1 NIV*

Upon hearing the news of her departure, the whole family gathered at Aunt Maribel's house where grandma's body laid. All her sons and daughters were able to hug and kiss her one last time before the morgue coroners came for her body. It was one of the most difficult moments we have ever experienced as a family. Everyone in the house cried with deep pain knowing that we would no longer have her by our side, that we could no longer feel her tender hugs that made us feel invincible, or hear her sweet voice telling us how much she loved us. At the same time, we were very grateful to God for the years we were able to enjoy an extraordinary mother and grandmother. Most of all, we were thankful that she was already in complete peace enjoying eternity with the one dear to her heart. Just seeing her on the stretcher, with her eyes closed and a beautiful smile, we knew that she was with Jesus, content, without pain, without any worries, in perpetual joy.

Many people say wonderful things about the special people in their lives, but in my case, Grandma Norma was more than special. Mama Norma, as many called her, was a pillar of faith for our family. Her faith and love for Jesus were her greatest legacies. Her prayers, wisdom, compassion and love for people will leave deep imprints in our hearts. A single piece of advice from Mama Norma changed the direction of many people's lives. A single hug from Mama Norma healed deep wounds of the heart. God used her embraces full of love and her words of wisdom to change and transform many families and marriages. People, who knew Mama Norma, affirm that her most powerful ministry were indeed her hugs; because through them we could feel the true love of the Heavenly Father. Thanks to her story and legacy many people were able to know about Jesus, our Savior.

Many will come to the Lord's presence because one day Mama Norma prayed for them or because one day, she gave them a simple hug or advice that made a difference in their lives. To this day, we continue to hear testimonies of people who have been blessed and changed by Mama Norma's testimony. Her legacy will continue, and as she always said, "all of my family will be saved, and all will serve the Lord."

Chapter 2

# The Beginning

Mama Norma's life was one filled with trials that led her to be an admirably strong and courageous woman. Norma Rodriguez Evangelista de Martinez was born on April 3, 1932, in Sabana de la Mar, a small town in the province of Hato Mayor del Rey, Dominican Republic. Her parents were Hipólito Rodríguez and Francisca Evangelista; Norma was the first born of eight children. Her father, Hipólito, was a farmer and her mother, Francisca, a housewife. Her brothers José, Silvio, Octavio, Ángel, Diógenes, and two sisters, Amantina and Rosa were very special in her life.

Norma was born into a Catholic home with a hard-working and loving family. Her father worked relentlessly to support his family in his work as a farmer. Thanks to her father's determination there was always food at home. All of their children were able to receive an education through sixth and eighth grade. At the time, education was not a priority due to great poverty and need. Many parents had no choice but to send their children to work at an early age to help with the household expenses. However, Norma was very fortunate to have had the opportunity to get an education especially because she was a girl and mostly boys were given the priority when it came to education. Norma studied up to the sixth grade in a public school in her town. Like many girls in those days, she had to learn to cook from an early age to help her mother prepare food for her older siblings. Her younger sister, Rosa, was very close to her throughout her life. Tia Rosa, as we all call her, was her best friend. They grew up very united and helped each other with household chores. Aunt Rosa remembers Norma as a very loyal and obedient daughter throughout her childhood. She helped a lot around the house and was always kind and hardworking.

In 1947, at the age of 15, Norma traveled from Sabana de la Mar to visit her cousin Josefina who lived in Hato Mayor, a countryside with lots of cattle and farms. During that visit she met a truck driver who was a friend of her cousin, named José Joaquín Martínez. He was a divorced man with two children who lived with his parents. Upon meeting Norma, Jose fell in love with her and traveled to Sabana de la Mar to ask for her hand in marriage. Seeing that he was a hard-working man from a good hardworking family, Norma's parents accepted his proposal. Norma was always very submissive and obedient. She accepted what her parents decided and the following year after a strict courtship, at the age of 16, she married her first boyfriend, José Joaquín Martínez.

Norma, a humble, obedient and hardworking young woman found herself in a very difficult situation when she had to marry someone who she didn't really know and who

14

was almost twice her age. They married in the Catholic church and began their new life together as husband and wife. After the wedding, Norma and her husband, Jose, moved in with her in-laws' in Hato Mayor. Jose's parents, his siblings and her husband's two sons, Jacinto and Luis also lived there. Norma quickly became a wife, mother, housewife and daughter-in-law. But the hardest part of all was the surprising realization that her new husband suffered from alcoholism.

The nights seemed never-ending as she awaited the arrival of her husband. Norma stayed up night after night praying and asking God to have mercy on Jose so that he would return home safe and sound. Her husband's job pertained of driving trucks and cars from city to city for deliveries and transportation, but very often after work he stayed in the bars washing his money away on alcohol. On several occasions Norma would go out in the middle of the night knocking door to door at every bar and nightclub in town looking for Jose to take him home. When he finally got home, Jose would arrive drunk and, on many occasions, verbally and physically abused Norma. This went on for many years. Every time it happened, Norma sought refuge in her sister and friend Rosa, who lived in Santo Domingo, the capital city, about 80 kms. away. On one of those nights that Jose arrived drunk, he hit her on the head with a large cooking pot. Thus, bleeding and wounded, Norma left the house in search of a public car to take her to her sister's home. When she arrived at Rosa's house, her entire family greatly worried for her. Her parents begged Norma to divorce Jose, but she refused. She stayed a few weeks at her sister's house to recover and rest. After a month or so, Jose arrived at Rosa's house looking for Norma and asked for her forgiveness. She forgave him and the next morning they returned home together.

Soon after, something special began to grow in Norma's heart. She couldn't explain it. She felt the desire to visit a Baptist church with her cousin Josefina. There, with the help of some missionaries visiting from the United States, she received Jesus as her Lord and Savior and began a beautiful relationship with her new love. Although she was raised as a catholic, she never really had a relationship with her heavenly father. She was raised with the customs and religious activities but there was never a heartfelt transformation. She always felt that something was missing within her. After this experience and receiving Jesus as her Lord and Savior, the church quickly became a very special place for her. There she learned from the Word of God, she learned how to pray and have communion with her Heavenly Father. She joined the choir of her Baptist church in Hato Mayor and participated every weekend singing hymns and choruses that filled her heart with peace and love. Her new relationship with Jesus filled her with the peace she so desperately needed. Her faith became the instrument that God used to help her endure the difficult situation that she faced daily with her husband and family. It was in moments of despair that Norma took refuge in the arms of her beloved Jesus, her Savior. Her daily communion with God was the strength that gave her the courage to keep on fighting for her family and well-being.

This new strength led her to believe that she could create a better future, since her husband did not take responsibility for their household. Norma gathered up her strength and decided to ask her father and brother Silvio for help. With a new vision for her life, she asked Silvio to help her look for wood, stones and cement to start building her new home, which became the great project of her life. She looked for a place near the cemetery of Hato Mayor, in an unoccupied land full of cattle. There she chose a spot and began to build

16

the house that would one day be a beautiful home for her family.

With the help of God, her father and siblings, Norma began to build a small house that she could call her own. They looked for soil, sand and cement to prepare the foundation. She walked nearly a mile to the river in search of stones that she carried on her back to strengthen the walls of her house. Day after day she walked back and forth from the river to the place where she was building her new home carrying barrels of water and dirt. She never gave up! At her young 20 years of age she became an admirably strong and courageous woman.

It had been seven long years since Norma married Jose. During all this time, she had not been able to get pregnant. Abuse, stress and long sleepless nights were not of good nourishment for her reproductive system. At the end of these seven years, more or less in the year of 1955, with the walls of her new home already up and with the roof of leaves covering her house, Norma discovered that she was pregnant. A few months later in the home she could finally call hers, she gave birth to her first daughter, Hilcia Esther (also known as Mercedita). Everyone called this child a miracle of God. During the delivery Norma had many complications. She nearly lost her life. Hilcia spent too much time in the womb because Norma was not advancing in centimeters to give birth. After many hours in labor and with the help of a midwife and her parents, Norma finally gave birth to her first daughter. The baby was purple and fragile from the long hours in labor and lack of oxygen. This beautiful baby girl paved the way for the rest of the children to come into the world one after another.

After her first birth, Norma got pregnant every year after that for the next 15 years. The immense happiness of having her new family could not extinguish the difficulties that continued daily in her home. Norma's second child and first son, Jose David, was born in 1956 and her third child, Jose Daniel, was born in 1957. Because her children were so young, it was impossible for her to return to work. Unfortunately, this worsened the financial situation in the household. Jose continued to binge drink instead of contributing to supporting his family. Not having the money to buy food for her children, Norma had to be resourceful. She had no other option but to go out to the streets and find a way to help feed her children.

Day after day she would go out walking in her neighborhood and around town with a baby in her belly and a trail of small children behind her, knocking door to door, offering her cleaning services in order to support and feed her children. Neighbors and people around the neighborhood would see her walking the streets with her little ones behind her as if they were baby chicks. People felt very sorry for her and offered her food for the little ones who cried unconsolably with hunger and thirst. Sadly, due to such great need and lack of nutrition, her fourth baby, Maria del Carmen, whom she carried in her womb died.

Chapter 3

# Psalm 37:25

In every tribulation and necessity, Norma clung on tighter to her great Heavenly Father. Her faith gave her the strength to keep fighting for her children. A year after the loss of her baby girl, she became pregnant again with her next daughter, Fatima. Many would ask, how could they continue to have children when they were in such great need? Well, in those days, many people didn't have access to contraceptives and weren't educated about planning pregnancies. Norma never really had a person to advise or guide her. She came from a very humble family and, in her great humility, she just did what she knew or understood was best. To go to a doctor, you not only needed the money to pay for the consultation; you also had to figure out how to pay for the prescription, should it be necessary. The practice of home medicine prevailed at that time, which was something that favored many low-income families like Norma.

In 1959, Norma gave birth to her fifth child, Fatima. Previously, she had lost a baby girl. So, the arrival of Fatima, a beautiful baby girl, became very special for her and for the entire family. By this I do not mean that the new baby girl replaced the baby she had lost. Knowing Norma, we know she would never forget her. Thank God, Fatima brought joy back into the heart of a mother who was suffering the loss of a longed-for pregnancy.

Before her second birthday, Fatima became seriously ill with an intestinal disease. They went to the neighborhood clinic and prescribed medicine to eliminate the parasites growing in her little belly. Unfortunately, just minutes after giving her the medicine, Fatima lost consciousness. At that moment, seeing that her daughter was no longer responsive, Norma ran out of the house with her baby in her arms screaming for help. The neighbors came to her aid and looked for a car to drive her to her sister Rosa's house. Norma cried the whole way to the capital and asked God to have mercy on the life of her little daughter. With tears in her eyes, she finally arrived at her sister's house. She got out of the car with her almost lifeless baby in her arms. She fell to the floor and began to scream with such loud cries that it caused everyone in the neighborhood to come out of their houses to see what was happening. Rosa and her whole family ran to help Norma and her baby. Rosa quickly took the baby in her arms and realized that she was in very serious condition. Without thinking twice, they got on her husband's motorcycle and left immediately for Angelita Children's Hospital. When they arrived at the hospital, they transferred Fatima to intensive care to try to save her life. Devastatingly, the medicine they had previously given Fatima had poisoned her blood. They kept her in observation for a few days and when they saw that the baby had very little time left to live, Norma and Rosa decided to take her out of the hospital so they could return home to Hato Mayor.

They had to make this very difficult decision because if the baby died in the capital, they would not have the money to pay for the medical expenses and the ambulance to bring her home. The doctors did not agree with them taking the baby in such critical condition, but they felt they had no choice. Rosa had to fight the case and explain to the doctors that they didn't have the money to cover the expenses. They signed the papers to take full responsibility for the baby so they could take her home with them. During all this time, Jose, Norma's husband, who was working in the city near *Angelita*, never showed up at the hospital to give them his support. These were some of the most difficult and painful moments Norma had to live through. In tears and with her beautiful baby in her arms, accompanied by her sister Rosa, they arrived at the house to prepare for their trip to Hato Mayor. Upon arriving at Rosa's house before getting out of the car, they realize that the baby had died in Norma's arms.

"You can't cry, Norma! You can't cry!" Rosa tells her, covering her mouth so she wouldn't scream and so that no one would realize that the baby had died. "If they see that the baby has died, they're not going to let us leave for Hato Mayor! Norma, do you understand me?" Norma, finding strength where she didn't have it, wiped the tears from her eyes and got out of the car with the baby wrapped in a blanket to enter the house. Once inside, Rosa quickly took the baby and ran to take Norma to the bathroom so she could scream and cry there. She cried inconsolably, covering her mouth with a towel so no one would hear her pain-stricken screams. That same night they left in Rosa's brother-in-law's car for Hato Mayor. It was twelve o'clock at night when they finally arrived.

There, with her baby wrapped in her arms, she opened the car door and falling to the ground let out a heartbreaking cry that burst from the depths of her soul. It woke up the entire neighborhood. Family, friends and neighbors all ran out of their houses realizing what had happened. They entered the house and found Jose lying drunk on the floor. Rosa's brother-in-law and husband picked him up and sat him down. The whole neighborhood came in behind them; all together they mourned the death of the baby girl they loved so much.

The pain of losing her beautiful daughter was immensely difficult for Norma. I remember having a conversation with her around a year before her passing about the tribulations of her life. And I remember her telling me the story of Fatima still feeling the pain of losing her. She would tell me "the death of a child is a pain that I do not wish on anyone, not even on my worst enemy; it is a pain that is never forgotten." She never forgot that pain.

Only a few months after Fatima's death, in 1961 Norma gave birth to her next daughter. She named her Maria Fatima in honor of her two deceased daughters. After a few months she became pregnant again and gave birth to, Juan Felix, in 1962. After Juan's birth, she gave birth to her next daughter named Ruth Noemi. Sadly, the joy of having her children could not extinguish the difficult situation she was experiencing on a daily basis. Jose, her husband, continued his addiction to alcohol and everyone at home suffered greatly, especially the children. The entire burden of the home, the children and the finances were on Norma's shoulders. There is really no explanation as to how they were able to survive in the terrible situation in which they lived, but we do know that God had wonderful plans for Norma and her children. There were days when they had nothing to eat, but also days when someone would show up at their door, a neighbor, a friend, or a relative with food to feed the whole family. God never forgot her. Her prayers and great faith kept her with a strong spirit and she never stopped fighting for her family. That is why she always recited her favorite verse to us with such certainty, because that was truly what she lived. God never forsook her.

"I have been young, and now am old;

yet have I not seen the righteous forsaken,

nor his seed begging bread."

Psalm 37:25

Because of the great poverty they lived in, the children were constantly falling ill. After the birth of her daughter Ruth Noemí, in 1966 their fourth son, Panguito, was born. Panguito was born with a disability. When he was one year old, they realized that he could not walk properly. He would crawl on the floor instead of walking. His little legs were very weak and could not support his weight. The family continued to grow and a few months later, in 1967, another son, Cristobal Joas, was born. Everyone at home helped each other because Mom was always busy with the baby and the younger ones. So, the older ones, especially big sister Hilcia, had to take care of her little siblings. She was like a second mother to all of them. Since Panguito could not walk, the siblings worried more for him. They all helped each other and were very close. At his young age of 3, Panguito became very ill. The doctors told Norma that he would not live long because of his condition and after a few months he died. This death became the third loss for Norma and her family.

Shortly after the loss of her son Panguito, Norma was pregnant for the last time. In 1969, she gave birth to a baby girl who brought much joy to the family and they named her Maria. She was a sweet child who brought so much laughter and happiness. However, given their extreme poverty, illnesses never ceased at home. If it wasn't the children who got sick, it was Norma or her husband, Jose. Life was not easy for her; it was a constant battle. As we already know, Norma never stopped fighting for the well-being of her family. At about 3 or 4 years old, the youngest daughter, Maria, her daughter Ruth and her son Jose Daniel became seriously ill with stomach parasites causing chronic diarrhea. These three children became more ill than the others and as they did not have the money to seek medical help, Norma would make home remedies to relieve their pain. One day, the remedies were not helping, and the chronic diarrhea would not stop. With the difficult situation at hand, Norma asked for help from her neighbors. She asked that they take her to her sister Rosa's. When she arrived at her sister's town, Norma, with her nerves on edge, could not remember her sister's address and asked her neighbor to drop her off at the local Radio station called *Guarachita*. Upon arrival she was able to convince the radio station to send a message over on-air to her sister.

Rosa's relatives heard the call on the radio and informed her that her sister was waiting for her at the radio station. Rosa with the help of her brother-in-law immediately went in search of Norma. Rosa found her and the children at the station with their clothes drenched in feces. The smell impregnated the entire radio station. Tia Rosa shared the story with me and told me that as soon as they arrived home, she put them in the bathtub so they could bathe and get rid of the stench and fatigue they carried. She fed them and gave them a home remedy to stop the diarrhea. The next day, they were taken to the hospital where they received medical attention and, a few days later, were healthy and ready to return home. Tia Rosa was truly the angel that God used time and time again to save Norma. What would Norma have done if it weren't for her sister? God knew how much she needed Rosa in her life. We thank God for the life of Tia Rosa who was such a special instrument for the wellbeing of Norma and all her children, truly a sister like few others in the world.

Chapter 4

# God's faithfulness

Norma was a tremendous fighter. Everything she faced in her marriage and with her children was truly extraordinary and unimaginable, but all of it was only the beginning of her story. There is so much more to learn about her life and what made her a true hero for the entire family.

Twenty-six years of trials, storms, pain, sickness and death passed; living and fighting day after day without fainting. 1975 was the year that marked and changed everyone's life forever. That year, at the age of 59, Jose Joaquin, Norma's husband and the father of her 11 children, died. At the age of 42, Norma was widowed, and lived with her children by her side in the house she had built with her very own hands. During all their years of marriage, José Joaquín had struggled with alcoholism. It was a very tough battle that sadly caused the family much pain, lack and sadness. Due to his heavy alcohol consumption for so many years, Jose was bedridden, his liver was severely affected with cirrhosis. During his last months of life, Jose was in very delicate health, but always surrounded by his beautiful family. There, on his deathbed, Norma shared the good news of Jesus with him again and it was there that Jose finally accepted Jesus Christ into his heart as his Lord and Savior. Norma's greatest heartfelt request during all the years of their marriage was that her husband would surrender his life to Jesus. She never grew tired of telling him about the God she served, the God who never forsook her, the God who always provided even when he, as her husband and father of her children, could not. She always spoke of that God who delivered her from death day after day, of that God who embraced her with great and pure love when her children died in her arms. She never wearied of speaking of the great and powerful God who had mercy on her life and that of her children. How could she not love her heavenly father? These are the lyrics of one of her favorite songs... "How could I not believe in God, if He has given me children and life, How could I not believe in God, if I feel Him in my chest every moment, how could I not believe in God?"

During that difficult time, her eldest daughter Hilcia was 19 years old. She experienced firsthand and witnessed all that her mother suffered and struggled with her father. Despite all that she lived through and witnessed between her parents; she always had a special love for her father. On many occasions, Hilcia had to accompany her mother to the bars looking for Jose to bring him back home safely. She was, in many ways, her mother's right hand. She always helped at home with the children by taking care of them so that her mother could go out in search of work and food for her family. No matter what her father was like, she always honored him by giving him the place in her life as her Dad. Whenever he came home,

Hilcia would run to get him clean clothes and shoes. Even when everyone was already sleeping late at night, she would wait up for him to make sure he arrived safely. She listened to the stories he told her about his travels to different towns and cities with such interest and love. She would comb his hair and laugh at his jokes. To Hilcia, her father was her best friend and she loved him with all her heart even with his mistakes and failures.

A few days before he died, her father sent for her. He took her by the hand and said: "Mercedita, you are going to get married one day. Yes, you are going to get married, but not to the boyfriend you have now, but to Fernandito, the one who came to visit from New York. If you marry your boyfriend my bones will tremble in the grave with sadness, but if you marry Fernandito, my bones will tremble with joy." A few days after that conversation her father died. Hilcia was left with those words engraved in her mind and heart. Fernando was the cousin of her neighbor whom she had met and seen just a few times. She never really had any type of relationship with him except for the cordial, casual and friendly greeting. But one night while she was sleeping, an angel appeared to her in her dreams and said "Mercedita, Mercedita, yes you are going to marry, but not with your boyfriend, you will marry Fernandito." At that moment, she awoke greatly surprised and afraid she ran to wake her mother. She told her what she had dreamt, and Norma said, "Hurry up! Break up with your boyfriend and reply to Fernando! Tell him yes!"

Days after her father's death, Fernando, her neighbor's cousin, had written her a letter declaring his love for her. In those days, Hilcia was confused and struggled with thoughts about what to do, but that dream was the confirmation she so desperately needed to act on the words her father had already expressed to her. Without hesitation, she finally broke up with her boyfriend and wrote a letter to Fernando telling him that she agreed to be his girlfriend. Two weeks after receiving the letter, Fernando traveled from New York and showed up knocking on the door with an engagement ring to ask for her hand in marriage. She accepted! And just like that, a few months later they were married in a church and had a spectacular wedding! Even in the midst of her poverty she was able to invite her entire family, neighbors and friends. A very dear friend of hers, named Sara Genao, offered to be the godmother of the wedding and went out of her way to make her dream wedding come true covering all of the expenses.

Fernando and Hilcia became an example to follow for the whole family and for all those who witnessed this beautiful marriage. They quickly began the paperwork so that Hilcia could travel to the United States. Fernando returned to New York to continue working while waiting for his new wife's documentation. After a few months had passed, Fernando returned for his beautiful wife to take her to live in the United States with residency. This was another example of the many ways God's hand was seen working in their lives to save and care for the entire family. God's faithfulness was very special over their family. God was fulfilling His promises in them.

Saying goodbye to her daughter was very difficult for Norma, but she had the great certainty that everything was entirely God's work to bless her family. For Hilcia it was extremely difficult as well, as she did not really know her new husband and was now going to live with him to another country far away from her family. But throughout the process, they both had their trust in God and His promises of provision for their family. Upon arriving in the United States, Fernando got Hilcia a job with the jewelry company he worked for. She began to work hard to support her family to eventually begin travel arrangements for her mother and siblings.

Hilcia, by God's great faithfulness, was already in the United States with her husband. Norma stayed with her other children and family in the Dominican Republic. She continued working and serving God while waiting for her daughter to submit the documentation to the Immigration Department so she could travel to the United States.

One night, as Norma and her youngest daughter Maria were walking home from church, halfway home they were surprised to see three women at the bus stop. It was already very late at night and there were no buses running at that hour. As Maria and Norma approached, the women asked Norma if they could stay at her house just for the night. Since they had no place to stay and Norma had a big heart, she said yes. The women walked with them the rest of the way home. When they arrived, Norma offered them food, but they kindly declined and told her they weren't hungry. Norma kept insisting because she wanted everyone to feel right at home. Norma took care of them with much love.

It was already very late and everyone at home went to bed. The three women spent the entire night singing and worshiping God from midnight until six in the morning. Norma got up early to offer them breakfast. When she entered the living room, she was surprised to see that they were no longer there. No one had heard the door open and no one noticed when the women left. But they did leave a sweet aroma of a pleasant perfume throughout the house. There Norma realized and greatly believed that these women were angels. Just as the word says, she had hosted angels in her home without realizing it. She said to her daughter "Maria,

30

you see! We should never stop hosting people in our home, because you never know if the person you will receive is an angel from heaven."

Another example of God's faithfulness in Norma's life was in 1978. Again, God demonstrated His power in her life. During those days, Norma sought every day to be closer and closer to God. She spent days and hours praying and seeking to learn and know more about the One who was dear to her heart. She congregated in a Baptist church where she and a group of women prayed for the sick. There was a young woman from the neighborhood named Candy. Everyone knew her because she was greatly possessed by demons. Her mother ran from church to church desperately seeking help and deliverance for her daughter. No one could fight the demons that tormented this young woman. Possession was something that had not been seen in this small town. The girl possessed and out of control repeatedly said that she would kill her family. She refused to eat or drink for days at a time. No one could control her or do anything to help her. Afraid for her life, her mother kept Candy locked in a room in the back of the house. Someone from the church told Mama Norma about this young girl's case. Norma felt strongly in her heart to help this family. Through prayer and fasting she prepared for meeting Candy and felt from God, when it was the right time to visit her at her home.

Accompanied by two sisters from the church, Mama Norma arrived at young Candy's house. When the mother opened the door, she asked Norma "Do you think you will be able to help my daughter? I have already taken her to many churches, and no one has been able to do anything for her." Norma answered "Yes" with great certainty and her warm hands filled with the power of God, "In the mighty name of

Jesus, Yes we can! Let us in!" The mother showed them where she had the young woman locked up; she had her in the last room in the back of the house. With great fear, the mother removed the padlock from the door so they could enter. Upon seeing Mama Norma, the young woman immediately began screaming uncontrollably and threw herself on top of Norma attacking her. Norma grabbed the young woman by the arms and with great authority pushed her against the wall. She held her with all her strength and began to rebuke and cast the demons out of her. The other women helped hold her, supporting in prayer. There, praying aloud with God's delegated authority, they did not stop until the young woman was completely delivered. The young woman began to vomit and cry. She began to take deep breaths and finally came to. "What happened to me, where am I? I'm so hungry!" As they heard her speak, they all began to give glory to God for the miracle of deliverance in this young woman's life.

The news of this great miracle quickly spread throughout the neighborhood. Everyone was filled with amazement at the great work God had just done with the young girl, Candy. To the glory of God, she was completely healed and free. She gave her life to Jesus and began to serve Him wholeheartedly. She became a Sunday school children's teacher at the church where Mama Norma congregated. Candy was never the same! Only God could do what He did in Candy's life and He will continue to do it for others today and forever.

God's protection was always with Norma and her children. God always showed his faithfulness in their lives and in their families. From her oldest daughter's marriage onward, they never lacked anything. Thanks to God's daily provision and her job in New York, Hilcia was able to send money to Norma on a monthly basis to help with their expenses. Every step was delicately orchestrated by God to take care of her and her children. A few more years had passed and in 1984, Norma was finally asked to take up residence in the United States. This blessing was another sign that God was with her. God's faithfulness greatly marked every season of Norma's life. And this new stage was one of the greatest moments in her life.

Chapter 5

# God's Promises

In 1984, at the age of 52, Norma made one of the biggest decisions of her life. She decided with a heavy heart to leave her children behind to travel to the United States in search of a better life. Norma joined the list of so many people around the world who have had to make the same decision in search of better opportunities for their families. This is a deep, but very necessary pain and many have no other choice. Had it not been for God's protection and provision over her life, she would never have made it to age 52. Norma's life was truly a miracle of God. She never gave up until she had achieved all of her dreams and desires and, above all, saw God's purpose and promises fulfilled in her life.

Her trip to the U.S.A. started a new beginning for Norma. She was lovingly welcomed into her new home with her daughter Hilcia and son-in-law Fernando Carrion, in Queens,

New York. Norma arrived a frail, weak, and malnourished woman with no idea what God had planned for her future. In a short time, she prepared herself to look for work by taking classes to become a home health aide. She quickly began working with an agency and was assigned to an elderly couple. Norma grew passionate about her job and became another daughter to the elderly couple she served. She lived with and cared for these beautiful seniors for ten years. And during all this time, she saved enough money to send her children an allowance and continue to maintain the home she fought so hard to build. Together with her daughter Hilcia, she started the residency process to bring her entire family one by one with their spouses and children to the United States.

Norma could see God's hand at work in her life, turning her great dream into a reality. Who could have imagined such a great blessing after so much suffering and pain? Only God! Only God can do what He did in her life. A transformation from death to life with an irrevocable destiny, calling and purpose. When she thought it was her end, it was really only her beginning. A new beginning, a new horizon, a new dawn for Norma Martinez. Each of her sons, daughters, their spouses and children, all arrived in New York through God's great promise and the words that came out of her husband's mouth to her oldest daughter before he passed away; "Mercedita, you are going to get married one day, but not to the boyfriend you have now, but to Fernandito the one who came to visit from New York." Those words and the confirmation of God through an angel in a dream so that the marriage of Fernando and Hilcia would be fulfilled, were all part of an amazing strategic plan of God for the love of Norma; for the love of Mama Norma, the beloved daughter of Jesus.

Since her arrival in New York, she began to congregate with Hilcia and Fernando in the Pentecostal church Lirio de Los Valles and there she served the Lord as a deaconess and counselor along with Pastors Juan and Marta Caraballo. Passionate about Jesus, Norma only wanted to know more and more about Him every day. Everything that came out of her mouth was the Word of God. Jesus became her great passion. Her life was an example of being the hands and feet of Jesus on earth. Her ministry became about transmitting the love of the Father through advice and prayers. She visited prisons and hospitals, always praying for the sick and setting the captives free.

In 1988, Lirio de los Valles ministry became Centro Cristiano Adonai. There she worked hand in hand with the new Pastors Frank and Rosemary Almonte. Her passion for souls and families grew each and every day. Norma gave her life to the service of God. Everything she did, as the Word says, she did it as if it was for the Lord. She worked closely with Pastor Rosemary Almonte in the women's ministry. At the same time, she volunteered faithfully in the intercessory ministry praying for the needs of the ministry and families and visiting the sick in hospitals and homes. The fruits of the Spirit lived and shone in her; she reflected the pure love of God in her smile, in her words and especially in her hugs, always helping those in need without a second thought.

Norma remained active in ministry, strengthened in faith and in God's call on her life. She worked tirelessly in the intercessory ministry with her spiritual son, Jose Penton. Together they shook the kingdom of darkness in intercession with their powerful declarations and their great evangelistic influence. They won many souls for Christ. Everywhere she went, Norma won a soul for Jesus whether it was in the marketplace, medical office, beauty parlor, restaurant, on the streets, in a store, and in hospitals. No matter the time or place of need, she was always ready to offer the way to eternal life through Jesus Christ to anyone she came in contact with. The love that flowed from her words and her life was so convincing that she left people no choice but to receive Christ as their Lord and Savior. We know that it was the supernatural grace of Jesus that shone upon the life of my beautiful grandmother, Norma.

She lived so many wonderful moments with her family in faith. She served God with immense joy. She loved her Pastors Frank and Rosemary Almonte as if they were her own children and was a great blessing in their lives for many years. She was a faithful friend, mother and counselor to them. She was with them during the most beautiful moments as well as the most difficult moments of their lives. There were many laughs and happy moments, also moments where they cried together and supported each other in faith. The love between them was truly wonderful and never stopped being so. She worked alongside Pastors Almonte in raising a construction site in a very poor town called Bayaguana, in the Dominican Republic. Together with her daughter Hilcia, Jose Penton and other people from the ministry, they went to do missionary work, praying for the sick and feeding the hungry.

During her journey in the faith, her advice and prayers restored many marriages and families. She won many souls for Christ; many of them today are pastors, evangelists, apostles, prophets and teachers. She was a spiritual mother to many. Pastor Leonel Mateo was one of her many spiritual children who today are of great blessing to the city of New York. Her humility and heart for Jesus made her stand out among others. Many knew Norma for her great love for all.

She loved so many as if they were her own biological children. The love she gave to each person was truly supernatural. I often wondered; how could it be that one person could have so much love for others? And love without condition? The answer? It was the pure and genuine love of Jesus that lived in her. Over the years, we have heard powerful testimonies of how God through Norma's life freed, healed and restored many people. And today, as her granddaughter, I feel more than privileged to be able to share her wonderful story as a testimony that absolutely nothing is impossible for God.

During these wonderful years, Norma lived for a time with her daughter Hilcia in a small apartment in Corona, Queens, New York as she awaited the arrival of her children who were to travel from the Dominican Republic. When her youngest son, Cristobal arrived with his wife Carmen and young son Cristobal Jr. she decided to move in with them to also enjoy their company as she had done with her daughter, Hilcia. She lived with them from 1992 to 2005. It was a delight to be able to share moments of her life with her children and grandchildren. She lived the next few years again with her daughter Hilcia and family. She always wanted to remain close to her family and that she did. Her life was of service to God and her family and she did it all with an immense love and passion.

In 2011, after 27 years, Norma decided to close the chapter of her life in the Adonai Christian Center, to join her daughter Hilcia Carrion and family to congregate in King Jesus Ministry in Astoria, New York. I remember that this decision was extremely difficult for Norma. She had asked God for confirmation every day because she did not want to make any sudden decisions. Everyone who knew Mama Norma understood the great fear of God that was in her heart. Before making any decision, she would pray to the Lord. Her heart was to honor God with her life, with her feelings, and especially with her decisions. At the beginning of a new season in her life, she fully trusted that God had everything in His hands. And as always, she gave what was left of her days to serve her heavenly father withholding nothing.

Wherever she went, Norma left her footprints of love and wisdom. Every person who approached her was filled with the sincere love that came from the love of her life, Jesus. She was a great blessing in King Jesus Ministries in New York with Pastors Leo and Liliana Gomez. There she continued working and serving the people for seven years, praying, counseling families, marriages and showing the eternal love that lived within her to bless everyone who surrounded her. Those hugs were also widely known in this place. Many lined up to receive one of those big special embraces. Those were hugs that literally healed and delivered. She gave herself so much to Jesus that her arms were faithfully used by him so that through them the heavenly father could embrace His children. Those were years of great blessing for Norma and for all those who shared with her.

# Chapter 6

# A New Opportunity

2017 was a year of great challenges in Norma's life. At the age of 85, she no longer had the same strength as before. She now walked slower and grew tired easily. However, we never thought that our beautiful grandmother and beloved mother, and daughter of God would receive such a horrible diagnosis. One Sunday in January while sitting in church listening to the sermon, she began to feel a small ball under her left arm very close to her breast. It bothered her a little, but she never thought it was something malignant. I remember that same day she told me when she got home after the service about the ball she had felt under her arm. I put my hand on it to feel it and certainly I did feel a small round growth. The whole family naturally became concerned and we made an appointment with her primary care physician, Dr. Lodha. Upon arriving for her appointment, the doctor completed a regular breast exam and felt a small mass. She was quickly referred to the specialists in oncology.

Mama Norma, as we know, was a tremendous woman of faith, but like many people these things about hospitals and doctor's appointments made her extremely nervous. Every time she had a doctor's appointment, she would get so nervous that she couldn't sleep all night. She would spend the whole night thinking, praying and declaring herself healthy. On the day of her appointment, the oncologist performed a mammogram and then a biopsy. Upon receiving the results of the biopsy, all of the doctors were surprised to see a woman so advanced in age with breast cancer. The news was very difficult for all of us, as she was the pillar of our family. Although it was certainly difficult news for her, her trust was placed on the rock that was Jesus and she always told us, "My children, my life is safely hidden in Jesus." Norma thought a lot about the welfare of her children and family and recognized the pain that this illness caused them. They did not want to see her suffer. However, she consoled them by telling them that, if this was her time, she would happily go into the arms of her beloved Jesus.

Norma, being a woman of great faith put her life in God's hands and allowed the doctors to do their job. They decided that the best option would be to remove her left breast in order to get the cancer out by the roots. They also recommended chemotherapy to continue to eliminate the cancerous cells, but Norma refused. She did not want to expose her body to radiation and decided to just have the partial mastectomy and take the cancer-fighting medication for five years. With her decision made, she was sent to a cardiologist for heart tests to see if she was in a good enough condition for this delicate surgery. Seeing that her heart was fine, they went ahead with the surgery plans. We had a few issues with the insurance process and also with finding a surgeon who would agree to perform the partial mastectomy. Due to her advanced age, many doctors did not feel confident in performing the procedure, but thanks to her granddaughter, Claribel St. Victor, and a long-time friend named Dayira, they were able to find an excellent surgeon to perform the procedure. Dayira worked at a hospital and knew a surgeon at NYU Langone Hospital. Dr. Susan Sanjohn, a surgeon with more than 25 years of experience heard Norma's story and lovingly took her case. This doctor was the instrument that God used to be able to achieve and move forward with the whole process of the mastectomy.

Finally, in March, two months after she felt the little mass under her arm, the insurance approved the partial mastectomy with Dr. Sanjohn. I remember the day of the surgery. It was a bit of a cold day in New York. The entire family, and her family in Christ, were lifting up prayers so that God would give her the victory through surgery. Naturally, Norma was very nervous. She had never had an operation as delicate as this one. On the way to the operating room she prayed in the spirit and said "Father, my life is in your hands." I have no doubt that there were angels by her side during the entire procedure. Even with her nerves on edge, she could feel an amazing peace. As she was being prepped for surgery, her sons, daughters and grandchildren waited in the waiting room. There we prayed together and declared that God's hand was guiding the doctors. We knew that God was her surgeon in excellence and that she was going to be just fine.

The operation lasted approximately five hours. With each passing hour it was even more difficult to wait. For us, those five hours felt like an eternity. We looked at the clock every minute, and every minute felt like an hour. At the end of the surgery, they transferred her to another room to monitor her while she woke up. We were all very anxious to see her. Dr. Sanjohn came into the waiting room to give us the news that everything went well during the surgery. We were crying tears of joy thanking God for letting us have her for a little while longer. When she finally awoke, she was a little disoriented and in a lot of pain. That same night, she was transferred to the recovery room. And with each passing day she felt more strength and less pain. The doctors found her to be doing very well and congratulated her on such a quick recovery. Within a week she was discharged and returned home with her family. God, in his sovereignty, had given her a new lease on life so that she could enjoy her family like never before.

Two weeks after returning home, she had a follow-up appointment with her oncologist. Dr. Chaudhri reported that Norma had recovered well. The cancer had been completely removed with the mastectomy and the doctors were happy with the success of her surgery. Norma was feeling better every day and thanked God for giving her the strength and health to go on with her life. Every day she enjoyed her children, grandchildren, family and friends more and more. And the praise to God never ceased to come out of her mouth. Now more than ever she could preach and speak about the greatness and faithfulness of God in her life. Wherever she went, she proclaimed the good news of salvation with great joy and love and told her testimony of how God had delivered her from death. She was full of peace and hope looking forward to the future with great expectation of what God now had planned for her and her family.

Chapter 7
# Difficult Changes

New York City was very special for Mama Norma. As much as she loved her homeland, New York had become her refuge, offering a better living standard than she ever thought possible. Now, after 35 years of creating a beautiful life with her children in this city, she was presented with the opportunity to move to Miami, Florida with her daughter Hilcia and family. This opportunity became another very difficult decision for her.

As we already know, Mama Norma was a woman of great faith, passion and love. Her relationship with God was truly admirable. There was no decision she could make big or small without first presenting it to God in prayer. When we talked to her about the idea of moving to Miami, she listened to everything without saying a word. I remember as we showed her pictures of the houses we wanted to buy and the beautiful neighborhoods we wanted to visit, she would just pucker her lips and say "Aha...that's nice." She hesitated to make the decision as she did struggle with the idea of leaving her children and family again.

Those were days when she didn't talk much, she was always very reflective. If we asked her what she thought about the idea of moving, she would only say with sadness in her voice ,"Let's see what the Lord says." Her love for her children and family was always very great. Her family and children were her life after God and the thought of being away from them again caused her great sadness.

I remember her saying to me, "Rusa, a mother's love is so big. My children need me." However, I think *she* really needed them. Her biggest concern was not being near her children and not being able to see them or visit them whenever she wanted to. She recognized that, when she left, everything would change and that caused her a lot of fear. Two months passed and it was time to decide what she was going to do. Many family meetings were held. Meetings with each of her children and families to see what they thought about the idea of having Mom a little far away. We looked for other options in which she would feel happy and at peace, but in the end the decision was entirely hers.

Each of her children had their own family situations and many did not have the comforts in their homes that she needed. And as an intelligent and knowledgeable woman, she looked at each of her options and prayerfully presented them all to God. After a time of prayer and fasting, she called another family meeting to present the final decision she had made. The idea of change was difficult for Norma because at

86 years of age, she realized that this might be her last good-bye.

With God's strength, she gathered her children one night and told them all the news that she had made the difficult decision to move to Florida. With tears in her eyes, she explained to them how she felt in her heart about having to leave them, but that she was certain it was the best decision for her at the time. She explained that it took her a long time to think and pray, waiting for God's confirmation. And after waiting on God, she received the "yes" for this new season of her life. Everyone welcomed her decision and recognized that it would be the best option for her. This decision left some of her children very unsettled because they imagined that it could be the last time, they could have her around, but they all trusted in God. If God was in the matter, she would be well and happy in her new home.

All goodbyes are very sad, even if they are for the best. In the last few weeks before moving we took the time to say goodbye to each of our family and friends. We visited Adonai Christian Center to say goodbye to a very special family for Mama Norma. It was a beautiful time that we could see the love and appreciation that everyone had for our beautiful mother and grandmother. We felt so much peace and confidence in this new beginning. As the days approached, Norma felt even more peace because God was holding her hand, just as He had held her hand all of her life. She felt a familiar peace, the peace that surpasses all understanding was upon her. There was no doubt that God was with her at every season of her life and especially during this last one.

June 29, 2017, was the day we left New York for our new home in Miami, FL. We were all leaving very happy and expectant for what God had instore for us in this new state. It was my husband Freddy, my young daughter Sophia, my dad Fernando, my mom Hilcia and my beautiful Abuelita Norma. My uncle Juan Felix accompanied us to help with the move and I was five months pregnant with my son Stephen. Abuelita said goodbye to her family with many tears and pain in her heart, but at the same time happy to be with our family to experience the new blessings that God had prepared for us.

Norma lived wonderful days in Miami. She enjoyed sitting outside watching and listening to nature. Sitting on the porch looking up to the heavens, singing worship and talking to Jesus. The nature and the weather reminded her so much of her beautiful home country. She would talk to neighbors and share her faith with anyone who came near her. She really enjoyed going to church and sharing with the brothers and sisters in the faith. Always hungry to learn more and grow more in her faith and relationship with the Father. Anyone who met her fell in love with her. She always showed God's love wherever she went. And as the months went by, she missed her children very much and talked to them on the phone every day.

A few months after her first year in Miami, Norma began to feel a lot of pain in her body and in her bones. The doctors told her it could be arthritis and for a month she took pain medication, but it was not enough to ease the pain. We decided to take her to the emergency room for further tests to see what was going on in her body. There, we were given the terrible news that the cancer cells had spread rapidly throughout her body, metastasizing only two years after her partial mastectomy.

After that devastating news, everything started to happen very quickly. Her body began to deteriorate rapidly. The only thing she wanted was to be with her children again in New York. She wanted to have them all with her during the last moments of her life. She saved all of her strength to make the trip back. We traveled at the end of December 2018. I remember the look in her eyes the moment she sat in the airplane seat. A look of relief and peace. She took us by the hand and said "Thank you Rusa and Maria for all of your help. God is with us and all will be well." When she arrived at her daughter Maribel's house, all of that strength disappeared. She was saving the last bits of strength to be reunited with her family in New York. She was very happy to see her children, her grandchildren, her sister Rosa and family. They were all able to enjoy her those last days. A few days after her arrival in New York she lost her appetite, the ability to talk and walk. On January 2, 2019, we took her to the hospital. The pain in her body was unbearable. The medications were very intense and had her asleep most of the time. All the family and brothers and sisters in the faith filled the waiting room and surrounded her bed with praise and prayers.

With only a few days in the hospital, hospice care was recommended to us. As a family we had to decide whether to do hospice care in the hospital or at home. Her children decided it would be best to have her at home and thus fulfill her wish to live her last moments surrounded by her family. We arranged transportation from the hospital to her daughter Maribel's home to give her the care she needed. What a difficult time that was! The journey was extremely hard and sad for us. Seeing her so frail and worn out broke our hearts. These were moments we never imagined we would see. When it comes to family you always hope and pray for the best. This was so heart drenching to experience. Finally, back home in her room with the necessary arrangements for hospice care, we sang worship songs and shared as a family the unforgettable moments we lived by her side. We hugged her, kissed her and cried all together. We grew closer as a family at her bedside. We enjoyed the last moments, even though she was no longer responding in any way.

That glorious morning surrounded by her daughters, on Friday, January 11, Mama Norma took her last breath with a smile full of peace. She passed away in the company of her beloved Jesus and left a huge void in our family. She left us with beautiful memories and beautiful moments that we will never forget. Although it was extremely difficult to experience her farewell, we recognized that the time to be in her heavenly home had come. That moment was the moment she had been waiting for and longing for. We know that it was the most wonderful moment in her entire life. She was finally reunited with the one she deeply loved and the desired of the nations, Jesus Christ. Today she sees us from heaven and rejoices to see the extraordinary things God is doing in and through us. We anxiously wait for the day that we can hold her again. Mama Norma, we will see each other again soon.

# Chapter 8

# Legacy of Faith and Love

*"But as for me and my house, we will serve the Lord."*
*Joshua 24:15*

$\mathcal{M}$ama Norma was a very special instrument in God's hands. She was created and designed by God with great purpose and calling. She had a special grace to influence all those around her. God had chosen her from her mother's womb to bring forth from her loins a blessed and separated lineage for His service. The God whom she served would be the same God whom her entire generation would also serve. Her greatest legacy was her faith in God and her love for humanity. My mother, Hilcia, always called her Mama Abraham because, just as Abraham was, she is the mother of generations. Because of her sacrifice, her covenant and love for Jesus, today her entire family is a blessed generation. We are covered under the covenant and promise she had with God. We believe that her prayers still cover us and reach us to this day.

I remember the times when Mama Norma would share her favorite Bible stories with us. One of the stories she loved so much was the story of two women who instructed their son in the ways of the Lord, Lois and Eunice. In the book of 2 Timothy, the Apostle Paul mentions Timothy's grandmother and mother, one of his closest disciples. In 2 Timothy chapter 1, the Apostle Paul writes to Timothy and tells him that he remembers that he is the son of a mother and grandmother with *an unfeigned faith.* These women had a good testimony because they trusted fully in God. Eunice and her mother in law Lois both received salvation and were a great influence on Timothy from his childhood. Although Timothy's father was Greek and his customs were different, Eunice decided to serve God and instruct her son in the ways of the Lord. From his earliest age, Eunice and Loida (the mother-in-law) guided and instructed Timothy in the fear and love of God. They taught Timothy the Word and guided him to be a man of great testimony and faith. Timothy grew up to become a great man of God and one of the Apostle Paul's most passionate disciples. He became a pastor in the church at Ephesus and preached the word of God throughout the world.

What did Eunice and Loida do? They passed on a great legacy of faith to Timothy better than any earthly inheritance. That genuine and pure faith was reflected in the lives of Eunice and Lois. They were women of prayer and great faith who influenced the people around them. The story of Loida and Eunice is very similar to the story of my grandmother

Norma and my mother Hilcia. Both women of great testimony instructed us in the faith; from a very young age we were all taught the Word of God, love for Jesus and service to him. Today, I am who I am because of the unfeigned faith of my grandmother, Norma and my mother Hilcia. They, like Eunice and Loida, persevered to the end without fainting. Although it was not easy, they remained faithful to the Lord. Despite the trials and many storms, they always remained steadfast in God's promises to their family. As it says in Joshua 24:15, Mama Norma always declared it, "...but as for me and my house, we will serve the Lord."

Besides the fond memories I have of my grandmother Norma, I also have beautiful memories of my mother, Hilcia, who was the director of the children's department at our church Centro Cristiano Adonai for more than 30 years. There, together with her, as little ones in our baby carriages, we learned of the word of God while she instructed the children in the faith. We sang praises and she taught us the importance of obedience and growing up as children with love and passion for Jesus. Children and their families would follow my mother wherever she spoke. Hundreds of children received Jesus because of her contagious passion and love. She would catch the attention of anyone with her fun and loving spirit. Those were truly incredible moments to witness, entire families came to the feet of Jesus during every children's service. Many children were healed, and countless of families restored! All because of Jesus!

My grandmother and my mother lived their lives for the service of the Lord and everything they did in and out of the ministry they did with pure and genuine hearts. Those memories are forever etched in my mind and heart. They, my mother and grandmother, were and always will be my greatest examples to follow. The best inheritance we can leave our children today is to lead them to have a real and personal relationship with Christ. We must be examples for our children so that they can one day do the same for the future generation. Because serving God is never in vain! You and your household can also serve the Lord. And that blessing will follow you forever.

Just like Jesus, Mama Norma left her footprints of faith and love in every heart and in every person throughout her life. Her wisdom, her hugs, her advice and prayers were incredibly special to so many! Those footprints today shine brighter than ever because through this book many more will be blessed with the testimony of her life and love for Jesus. I have no words to thank God for allowing us to share a piece of his heart here on earth with those who loved her. Although it was only for a short time, we were able to learn and enjoy so much from her. For all of her family, Norma is not dead, but alive. The Word of God teaches us that our physical body dies, but our spirit lives. Mama Norma lives today in her beautiful home, home sweet home, beyond the sun. She lives in our hearts and through each of her children, grandchildren and generations to come. She lives on through every teaching, through every piece of advice, every hug and every word of faith she gave us. Her memory lives on, her legacy lives on, her love lives on forever and ever.

Someday, the time will come when we will no longer be on this earth. Then it will no longer matter what assets you have or how much money you make. What truly matters is the legacy you leave here on earth. Have you ever wondered how you will be remembered? Do you think about how you can bless or influence someone in a positive way? You have to start paving the way today! Prepare yourself, prepare your soul, give your heart to Jesus and live your days for him. Because the day is coming, the day when in the twinkling of an eye we will be with Jesus. Prepare your life, so that on that day you will be ready. And then you will be reunited with your Creator. Everything will pass away in this life and the only thing that will remain is Jesus. Choose Him today!

Chapter 9

# Lamp at His Feet

*Mama Norma's favorite verses*

The word of God was truly a lamp at Norma's feet. She constantly recited and declared it aloud and always carried it close to her heart. Every day she woke up and read the book that transformed her life - the Bible. She always read it with great passion, dedication and love. She delighted in reading the words that strengthened her bones and nourished her being. The wisdom that flowed from her heart came from a place of searching and sacrifice. All that she could give came from the place of God's presence. She spent hours in her room reading, searching, learning and praying. She filled her Bibles with notes and her notebooks with revelation, questions and points for her studies. With all the years she had in the faith, she never stopped having a passion to learn more about Him. She always had a humble and genuine heart.

She longed to know more of her beloved Jesus and every day she fell more and more in love with Him.

That beautiful book and the words that stood out from its pages were pure life for Norma. When she read, those words flowed inside her and coursed through her veins. Her strength, wisdom, purity, passion and knowledge came from her surrender to God. She gave her life completely to Jesus who through natural men wrote that wonderful book. And today you too can change your life completely. You can surrender your life to find the eternal life that only Jesus can give you. If Norma could say what she would like to put in this book, it would be that everyone could receive and know the beautiful Savior who changed her life. The most important decision you can make today is to receive Jesus into your heart as the Lord and Savior of your life. Just as He did for Norma, He will do for you and your family. There is no problem too big for God to fix. You are very loved by your Heavenly Father. Come to him and you will never regret your decision. Repeat this simple prayer out loud,

*Jesus, thank you for your sacrifice on the cross for me. Thank you for loving me with an unconditional love. On this day I give you my heart and I receive you as the only Lord and Savior of my life. I repent of all my sins and run into your arms of love. Cleanse me with your precious blood and make me a new creature. Amen.*

If you prayed this important prayer, I invite you to seek a personal relationship with Jesus. You can do this by reading his word- the bible every day and simply talking to your creator. Find a place where you can learn more about him with people who will guide you in the faith; a church that believes in the power of God and preaches his word and truth. Just as babies need their parents to feed them milk, so does a new believer need someone to instruct them in the ways of the Lord. Congratulations on this new and wonderful season of your life! Never look back, keep your eyes on Jesus, trust that he is with you and he will guide you today and forever.

These verses were very special to my beautiful grandmother's life. They instructed her in her faith and guided her to be a great woman of God. I hope they will also be a great blessing to you. Walk and declare God's Word every day in your life and you will see the strength and health it will give to your mind, body and soul. Just as Mama Norma did, make that wonderful book a lamp unto your feet.

Here are a few of her favorite verses which she loved so dearly:

**Psalm 37:25 NIV**

I was young and now I am old,

yet I have never seen the righteous forsaken

or their children begging bread.

*\* Mama Norma stated this verse as a testimony of God's goodness in her life.*

**Psalm 1 NIV**

Blessed is the one

who does not walk in step with the wicked

or stand in the way that sinners take

or sit in the company of mockers,

but whose delightis in the law of theLORD,

and who meditates on his law day and night.

That person is like a tree planted by streams of water,

which yields its fruit in season

and whose leaf does not wither—

whatever they do prospers.

Not so the wicked!

They are like chaff

that the wind blows away.

Therefore the wicked will not stand in the judgment,

nor sinners in the assembly of the righteous.

For the LORD watches over the way of the righteous,

but the way of the wicked leads to destruction.

*\* Mama Norma would declare this chapter in the life of all her children and grandchildren every birthday. The best gift was the blessing of our abuelita on our birthday.*

## Psalm 119:105 NIV

Your word is a lamp for my feet,

a light on my path.

## Joshua 24:15 NIV

But if serving the Lord seems undesirable to you, then choose for yourselves this day whom you will serve, whether the gods your ancestors served beyond the Euphrates, or the gods of the Amorites, in whose land you are living. But as for me and my household, we will serve the Lord.

## Psalms 23 NIV

The LORD is my shepherd, I lack nothing

He makes me lie down in green pastures,

he leads me beside quiet waters,

he refreshes my soul.

He guides me along the right paths

for his name's sake.

Even though I walk

through the darkest valley,

I will fear no evil,

for you are with me;

your rod and your staff,

they comfort me.

You prepare a table before me

in the presence of my enemies.

You anoint my head with oil;

my cup overflows.

Surely your goodness and love will follow me

all the days of my life,

and I will dwell in the house of the LORD

forever.

## Jeremiah 29:11 NIV

"For I know the plans I have for you," declares the LORD, "plans to prosper you and not to harm you, plans to give you hope and a future.

## Galatians 2:20 NIV

I have been crucified with Christ and I no longer live, but Christ lives in me. The life I now live in the body, I live by faith in the Son of God, who loved me and gave himself for me.

## 1 Peter 2:9 NIV

But you are a chosen people, a royal priesthood, a holy nation, God's special possession, that you may declare the praises of him who called you out of darkness into his wonderful light.

## Proverbs 22:6 NIV

Start children off on the way they should go, and even when they are old they will not turn from it.

*\* Grandma Norma instructed her children in the ways of the Lord. Today her family and generation serve God.*

## Proverbs 31:10 NIV

A wife of noble character who can find?

She is worth far more than rubies.

*\*Norma was a truly virtuous woman.*

## Habakkuk 3:17-18 NIV

Though the fig tree does not bud

and there are no grapes on the vines,

though the olive crop fails

and the fields produce no food,

though there are no sheep in the pen

and no cattle in the stalls,

yet I will rejoice in theLORD,

I will be joyful in God my Savior.

## Psalm 91 NIV

Whoever dwells in the shelter of the Most High

will rest in the shadow of the Almighty.

I will say of the LORD, "He is my refuge and my fortress,

my God, in whom I trust." Surely he will save you

from the fowler's snare

and from the deadly pestilence.

He will cover you with his feathers,

and under his wings you will find refuge;

his faithfulness will be your shield and rampart.

You will not fear the terror of night,

nor the arrow that flies by day,

nor the pestilence that stalks in the darkness,

nor the plague that destroys at midday.

A thousand may fall at your side,

ten thousand at your right hand,

but it will not come near you.

You will only observe with your eyes

and see the punishment of the wicked.

If you say, "The LORD is my refuge,"

and you make the Most High your dwelling,

no harm will overtake you,

no disaster will come near your tent.

For he will command his angels concerning you

to guard you in all your ways;

they will lift you up in their hands,

so that you will not strike your foot against a stone.

You will tread on the lion and the cobra;

you will trample the great lion and the serpent.

"Because he loves me," says the LORD, "I will rescue him;

I will protect him, for he acknowledges my name

He will call on me, and I will answer him;

I will be with him in trouble,

I will deliver him and honor him.

With long life I will satisfy him

and show him my salvation."

*\* In the most difficult moments of Mama Norma's life, she took this word and trusted that God would take care of her and her family.*

## Matthew 22:37 NIV

Jesus replied: "Love the Lord your God with all your heart and with all your soul and with all your mind."

*\*Mama Norma was a living testimony of this verse. Truly, she loved Jesus with all her heart, soul and mind.*

## Joshua 1:9 NIV

Have I not commanded you? Be strong and courageous. Do not be afraid; do not be discouraged, for the LORD your God will be with you wherever you go."

*\* God was with her until her very last moment. God is faithful to his word.*

## 2 Chronicles 6:19-20 NIV

Yet, LORD my God, give attention to your servant's prayer and his plea for mercy.

Hear the cry and the prayer that your servant is praying in your presence.

May your eyes be open toward this temple day and night, this place of which you said you would put your Name there. May you hear the prayer your servant prays toward this place.

## Isaiah 58:11 NIV

The LORD will guide you always;

he will satisfy your needs in a sun-scorched land

and will strengthen your frame

You will be like a well-watered garden,

like a spring whose waters never fail.

*\* The word of God gave Mama Norma new strength every day.*

## 2 Corinthians 10:4-5 NIV

The weapons we fight with are not the weapons of the world.

On the contrary, they have divine power to demolish strongholds.

We demolish arguments and every pretension that sets itself up against the knowledge of God, and we take captive every thought to make it obedient to Christ.

## Ephesians 6:18 NIV

And pray in the Spirit on all occasions with all kinds of prayers and requests. With this in mind, be alert and always keep on praying for all the Lord's people.

*\* Grandma Norma prayed without ceasing. At any time of the day you could find her praying and worshiping her faithful friend, Jesus.*

## Philippians 1:21 NIV

For to me, to live is Christ and to die is gain.

*\* Mama Norma won a good fight and today she celebrates in heaven with her beloved Jesus.*

### Hebrews 4:16 NIV

Let us then approach God's throne of grace with confidence,so that we may receive mercy and find grace to help us in our time of need.

### Hebrews 13:1-3 NIV

Keep on loving one another as brothers and sisters. Do not forget to show hospitality to strangers, for by so doing some people have shown hospitality to angels without knowing it. Continue to remember those in prison as if you were together with them in prison, and those who are mistreated as if you yourselves were suffering.

*\*Mama Norma believed this with all her heart and on many occasions hosted angels in her home.*

### 1 Juan 2:10 NIV

Anyone who loves their brother and sister lives in the light,and there is nothing in them to make them stumble.

*\* Mama Norma lived this word. She loved everyone and always remained in the light.*

Chapter 10

# Traces of Love

*Testimonials*

Norma Martinez's life was a great blessing to every person who had the privilege of knowing her. She left traces of love in each of our hearts.

*Her legacy of faith and love will live on forever!*

**Testimony of younger sister Rosa Pimentel**

Norma was a wonderful sister. We were inseparable. I was the youngest in the family and Norma was my best friend. I received the Lord in my heart through her. She was my spiritual mother. I thank God for her life because she was a great example of a daughter, wife, mother and friend. I love you forever *Longo*.

## Testimony of her eldest daughter Hilcia Carrión

My mother was an excellent mother. An unforgettable woman. She loved her children very much with eternal love. She lived many years with my family and it was an honor to have her with me. She was my friend, my counselor, my love, my mother. I thank God for giving me such a beautiful mother. She fought for us. She always cared about getting ahead. She was a fighting warrior. She always did God's will wherever she went. She was a wonderful woman, an amazing wife, mother, woman of God. Her life was a life of service to God. When she hugged me and prayed for me I was healed. I am proud to be her first daughter. My mother's love was the best thing in my life. I miss her very much, but I carry her always in my heart. Thank you mom for all you did for me. I bless your life and I will never forget you.

## Testimony of her first son-in-law Fernando Carrión

Norma Martinez was an enterprising woman. Since she came to the United States, she never stopped working and fighting to support her children and bring them to this country. It was always a blessing to have her close to us. She was a mother to me. We really enjoyed worshiping God together and working in the ministry. We would go to the prisons once a month and pray for the prisoners. She was a tremendous woman of God.

## Testimony of Apostle Frank Almonte and Pastor Rosemary Almonte (Centro Cristiano Adonai Ministries)

In 1984 we arrived at the church, Lirio de los Valles where we met Norma Martinez (Mama Norma) and in 1988 when we started pastoring the church, she helped us and was a mother to us. She believed in our calling when others did not, and that pushed us to do more and develop the pastoral ministry.

Norma Martinez was a very humble and beautiful woman before the Lord. She always had a good spirit to serve and when she blessed us she would send us angels to take care of us. Mama Norma, as we called her, always had good advice in her heart for anyone who needed it. Her motherly love was shared among all of us. God gave us the blessing of working with her.

From the beginning of the ministry that the Lord placed in my hands and my wife Rosemary's in 1988, Mama Norma always supported our vision. She worked as a deaconess and after many years, as an elder. Her dedication was genuine and true. With godly fear and dedication, she did what the Father commissioned her to do. She was a great visionary preaching the gospel of the kingdom in the nations and building schools for children, especially in her native land, Dominican Republic.

We will always remember that great woman of God, MAMA NORMA. The Almonte family and Centro Cristiano Adonai will always honor and remember the one who blessed us greatly with her unconditional love. We thank God because we are sure that today she enjoys the company of our beloved, the Lord JESUS CHRIST.

## Testimony of her friend and spiritual son, José Pentón

Norma was a woman with God's heart. She was a mother, friend, counselor, mentor and spiritual mother. She was a great blessing to my life. Together we visited homes, hospitals and prisons. We traveled to missionary works in the Dominican

Republic. There we were able to evangelize, pray for the sick and feed the needy. Norma loved us all. If there was someone in need she was there to help them. She fought for the doctrine of Christ. The fruits of the spirit were visible in her and she lived to do the will of God.

### Testimony of María Tapia (friend of many years)

Mama Norma was everything to me. She was my mother, friend, and counselor. She gave me the love I never had. She knew all my secrets. She always gave me advice and never judged me. She loved me unconditionally. She was the only one who could calm me down when I thought I had had enough of life. Today I have a big emptiness inside. I miss her very much. I loved her with all my heart. She really was my mother and I gave everything for her. I even fought for her. The most beautiful thing that God did through Mama Norma was the union in my marriage. I lived with my boyfriend for many years without getting married. Mama always advised us to get married. The day of Mom's funeral we went back home very sad. My boyfriend came up to me and said, "I'm going to keep the promise I made to Mom." I wondered what that promise would be. Then he said "Let's get married!" After a few months we got married and for me this was a great miracle that God did thanks to Mama Norma. I love you forever Mama!

### Testimony of her youngest daughter, María Muñiz

Mom marked my life in all aspects because she was my greatest example to follow in her perseverance to God, in her love and in her devotion to God, her children, family and others. She had a big heart; she had the heart of God. But, above all, there are two things that Mom did that really marked my life.

When I was 15 years old, I would walk home from church with her. We walked for an hour to get to the church because it was far away. One night, in the middle of the road, we saw three women waiting at a bus station. Mom and I were surprised because it was very late at night and the bus didn't pass at that time. We approached them and when they saw us they asked if they could stay at Mom's house. They told her that it was only for that night because it was already late. Since they had no place to stay, Mom, in her kind heart, said yes. They came with us and when we arrived home, mom offered them food and they told her they were not hungry. Mom continued to offer them everything, because as a mom she treated everyone who came home as royalty. Mom took very good care of them. It was late and we went to bed.

The women spent the whole night singing and worshiping God from 12:00 midnight until 6:00 in the morning. Mother got up to offer them breakfast, but was surprised when she saw that they were gone. Only the great aroma of a pleasant perfume remained. There she realized that these women were angels. Mom sheltered angels in her house. She told me, "You see Maria, never stop hosting people in your house because you don't know who you will receive." That experience marked my life forever.

Another thing that struck me was that she never stopped giving her tithe and offering. Three weeks before she passed away she told me, "Maria, hand me that wallet. There is my tithe and offering; take it and put it in a King Jesus Miami church envelope and give it to them." And that's what I did. I put it in an envelope and brought it to the front and gave it because by that time I was taking care of her in Miami. She was faithful with her tithe and offering all the way through.

I should also mention that, in her last days, she had the names of her children in the fist of her hands and I asked her "Mom why don't you open your hand" and she said "No, no, no because my children are here and I can't let go." And she started naming them one by one with first and last name. She continued for hours and hours and then she opened her fists and said "Ready, I hand them over to you, Lord." She opened her fist and began to cry and that also marked my life because as a mother she wanted to protect her children. God cares for them and loves them more than we love ourselves, she said. As a mother, that was very powerful for me because now I have no fear. Mom always prayed and read the Bible every morning and raised her hands to God and thanked him for the new day and for his blessings. That was my beautiful mom. My queen and my unconditional friend.

### Testimony of her granddaughter, Noemí Martínez

Mama Norma, my Abuelita as she was called, was a woman full of God with much love, wisdom, grace and favor. She loved God with all her heart. She always prayed and interceded for her family and everyone. Wherever she went, she evangelized and won souls for God. She was a great example as a wife, grandmother and mother. I had the great privilege of having her in my home with my family for a few months. I remember that she always went to sit on the balcony to pray and thank God.

### Testimony of Niradey Perez

My dear mother Norma, through this message I want to thank you for your dedication to God's work here on earth.

She always had a wise word to say and a Bible verse to accompany each of her counsels. With a smile always on her face she showed a deep love for her beloved Jesus. On one occasion, I asked her why she had an engagement ring and she certainly replied; "Don't you know I am engaged? Yes! My daughter. I have a fiancé named Jesus and he is preparing a place in heaven and is coming for me soon." From then on a curiosity began in me to talk to her.

In her last days, I went to visit her with a bouquet of flowers to offer my support and encouragement, but to my surprise, she had a look of joy much greater than mine. At her bedside, she shared what God was showing her, in the end I ended up being ministered to by her passion for her beloved Jesus and said goodbye. She was always looking for someone to help even in her delicate state. One day while I was with her, she went to bed worried about the anguish she saw on my face rather than her situation. The next day, God revealed to her in a dream a concern I had. I hadn't told her anything. She said goodbye and said nothing to me as we said goodbye, but she sent me a message answering the request she had made to God in secret.

It was necessary to have met Norma Martinez. She cared for others before herself. I am a living testimony that Mama Norma in her last days was looking for what else she could do for her fiancé Jesus. Today I thank God for her life and hope to see her again soon to hug her, because I miss holding her and singing with her together to our beloved Jesus.

## Testimony of friends in the faith Orlando and Mayela Gudiel

We can fill books of beautiful memories of our sister Norma Martinez, spiritual mother, dear friend. A woman of good testimony, a counselor, a woman who knew how to give love, true and genuine, always available to those who needed her. A woman devoted to the service of God unlike any woman I have ever known, nor will ever know. I thank the Lord for having placed her at our side for many years. We will carry her in our hearts as long as we live. She was a tremendous blessing to my husband Orlando and me. We hope to see you in heaven one day, we remember you my beautiful friend! You will always live in our hearts.

## Testimony of her grandson, José Martínez

My name is Jose D Martinez. I am a first-generation grandchild of the honorable Norma Martinez who was considered the mother of many. My experience with my grandmother was a great blessing and influence in my life. Norma Martinez taught me to love and fear God, as the principle of having wisdom to conduct myself in this world. Her wisdom transcended boundaries, she was my primary counselor. I remember that since my childhood her prayers and declarations were always present in my life, she would often declare Psalms 1 over me.

In 1996, at the age of 16, I had an experience I will never forget, it was one of those missionary trips she did with her eldest daughter Hilcia Carrión; on that occasion it was in the city of Bayaguana, Dominican Republic, a city of great poverty; I was impressed by how she hugged those children in depressing conditions, I remember that she told me: Jesus died and rose again for them and brought us to show God's love with our compassion. My grandmother was an example in my life, she taught me to be grateful with the little or the much that we may have and to value the simplest things in life. She taught me to be humble, something she always mentioned to me was that she taught by example. On this mission trip for the first time I was able to experience what a missionary goes through to bring the bread of life that is Jesus Christ and provide clothing to the less fortunate.

She was very influential and instilled a passion for missionary work in me, so much so that today I am the director of the missionary group of my church "Enciende una Luz" (Let a Light Shine). By the grace of God, I have led two mission trips to Santo Domingo, Dominican Republic and we have plans to expand to other countries. I can say that the legacy she left in my life has been this; love for the less fortunate. Thank you, thank you very much, Norma Martinez for sowing into my life. If I were born again I would ask God to be with my beloved grandmother again. See you in heaven; pastor, counselor, missionary, mother. I love you grandma.

## Testimony of her son, José Mercedes

I was born with many stomach problems and different diseases. I was in constant pain. My mother always took care of me with lots of love. She would tell me "My son, as long as I am alive you will not die." We were 11 children and I would tell her "Mom, you have other children to fight for, let me go to God so you don't have to worry about me anymore." The pain was so unbearable that I would throw myself in front of the sand trucks so that they would run me over because I did not want to live with that pain anymore. My mother lived through all the suffering with me. She never left me nor forsook me. She always fought for me. Today my mother is with God and I thank God because she left me with 62 years of life. Just as she told me that I would not die; today I am alive because of her prayers and her great love for me. I love you mom.

## Testimony of her son, Juan Martínez

When I was 15 years old I developed a disease in which my knees filled with fluid and I could not walk. Mom would take me to doctors for help. The doctors said I would never walk again because the fluid could permanently damage me. Mom would search for different remedies to alleviate the pain I was in. Besides having that problem with my knees, I also got a skin disease with a severe rash. There was no remedy that would soothe the constant itching and burning I felt.

One day while I was praying and asking God to heal me, I saw a vision of a giant man coming towards me and touching my knees. I heard his voice say "Juan, from today you are healed." I ran to find my mother and told her what had happened. Sure enough, from that day forward I felt no more pain in my knees. Jesus had healed me completely! Our mother suffered a lot with us, but God was always with her. God never left us!

## Testimony of her daughter, María (Maribel) Martínez

My mother was a counselor and a very special friend to me. She was my everything after God. Mom was an inspiring woman. She was by my side in the most difficult moments of my life. When my husband got sick with cancer, my mother was my greatest help. She was always declaring the word of faith and strength for my life. She lifted my hands when I felt I could not take it anymore. Mom was with me hand in hand. She went with me every day to visit my husband in the hospital. He always felt good to see Mom come singing praises to Jesus. He was happy when he heard her voice. The day she didn't come to see him, he would be sad. Her voice conveyed peace and was like a balm for my husband. I became a widow with three children. God and my mother never left my side. I am grateful for the life of a tremendous woman who will always be my beautiful mother.

## Testimony of her daughter, Ruth Pizarro

I want to mention that Norma was not only my biological mother but also a spiritual mother of good testimony. She was a great friend and counselor. And I will always thank God for my mother. I remember that mom was always by my side. I was born with an illness in my stomach and she would run with me to the hospital. She suffered so much for me at that time. She was literally a mother of multitudes with eleven children. And she always gave the best of herself to each one of us. She gave us unconditional love and was like a hen guarding her chicks. I remember when I was fifteen years old I took care of her and worked to help her buy food. Mom had a humble heart and it showed in her actions, like when she cleaned the church and all of us always helped her. There were times when she would stop eating so that we, her children could eat. She is the picture of what it is like to have the heart of Jesus beating within her being.

## Testimony of her grandson, Eliezer Pizarro

Grandma Norma, wow, I don't even know where to begin. I am standing today because of her and my mom's prayers. I can admit I would be six feet under if it weren't for her prayers. But my Abuelita had faith in me and the man she saw that I could one day become. She believed in the God of heaven for my salvation. Today I am not only alive, but I bear a testimony of who God really is. And all because of her great faith in God and in me. I had the privilege of traveling to different countries with my spiritual father, Eddie James. Thank God I was able to have the blessing of her sitting down with me to tell me how proud she was of me in seeing me travel to the nations sharing the good news of what God did in my life and who God really is to me. She talked about how God can bring you out of nothing and make you a king alongside other kings.

Who is Mama Norma? She is the true definition of what it is to be a woman of God. I am blessed and privileged to be able to say that I am her grandson.

### Testimony of her son, José Jacinto Martínez

I was only 5 years old and my brother, Luis was 3 years old when our dad married Norma. She raised us with so much love while our dad worked and drank a lot. I remember her washing and ironing clothes in different houses to support and feed us. She did everything with so much dedication and love. In 1955, I was 13 years old when my sister Mercedita (Hilcia) was born. I helped her with the new baby and with my little brother, Luis, so she could continue working. Norma would prepare oranges and roast peanuts for me so I could go out on the streets and sell them. She would also go out to clean shoes to bring in money to help with the household expenses. When Norma started to build her house, Luis and I were there helping her look for the palms and stones to prepare the house. Always together, always united, always a family.

## Testimony of Pastor Leonardo Gomez (El Rey Jesus New York)

Mama Norma, beyond being a woman of God, with great wisdom, she was a mother who played the role of father and mother at the same time to raise her children. In addition, she was a pioneer so that her children and grandchildren would know the God with whom she had an encounter. Love was one of her great weapons to win back those who were lost. Something that struck me about this woman of God was the fact that regardless of the years she had in the gospel and her maturity, she was a woman submissive to authority because every time she went out to preach she gave an account and asked for the blessing of her covering. I end by saying this, there are few people like Mama Norma that leave their mark.

## Testimony of Pastor Liliana Gomez (El Rey Jesus New York)

It is a joy for me to speak of the testimony that Mama Norma left in me: from the first moment I met her, she impacted my life by her sweetness, her love for God and her love for people; always giving a smile, a sincere hug, a word of encouragement. She knew a lot about God and her gratitude to the Father allowed her to be an instrument in his hands to impart and give grace for what she had received.

I was very inspired by the confidence and security she had of being a true daughter.

A woman full of wisdom, with the word of God always in her mouth; she knew how to leave a legacy not only in her generation, but to everyone who knew her, a mother who lived to the fullest, and without selfishness. For me she was a great role model and example to follow. She showed me her love every time she invited us to her house and cooked us that delicious sancocho soup, which no one has ever been able to surpass. I could see the love and excellence with which she prepared it, she made us feel very special.

That was Mama Norma, a woman so loved by God that she left a little bit of herself in every heart that had the privilege of knowing her. Mama Norma; you will always be in my heart!

## Testimony of the Lara family - Nydia (Martha), Atanael and Carmen

Mama Norma, as many know her, was a blessing from God, with a heart of gold. Ever since I came to this country, she has been a blessing in my life. But the biggest thing she did for me, that I have always had in my mind was when she gave me her blessing to come out of a crisis. The experience I have with Mama Norma is that she was my salvation. I was the partner of one of her sons and we were in a domestic violence relationship. During the time I was with her son, things went from bad to worse, to the point that even the police had to intervene. The policeman then advised me to stay away from this situation, otherwise, either my partner would go to jail or my two children would be taken away from me. I didn't want to take action without telling Mama of my final decision. My concern at the time was that I didn't know what to do.

I remember that she supported my decision and told me that I should leave so that I could live a better life. This way, I would neither create more problems for myself with her son, nor risk making an extreme decision, nor put my two children in danger, and at the same time keep peace with the family. I liked her answer because as a mother and a woman, she did not favor her son. But as a Christian person, a child of God, and with good feelings she told me "Daughter, I can tell you that the best thing you should do is to take the opportunity to go where my son can't find you. This way you will give my grandchildren the opportunity to live in peace." After her advice, she told me to let her know of my decision and that she would support me financially. If it weren't for her, I would not have been able to move from one place to another. What I appreciated the most was that she kept our conversation a secret. The only thing she asked me was not to tell anyone, not even her, of where I decided to move to. There were more situations where she offered to help me and my children, I thank her with all my heart for what she did for my family. I will never forget her.

## Testimony of her youngest son, Cristóbal Martínez

My mother was a hardworking woman. She ironed, washed and planted cilantro so I could go to the market and sell it when I was 9. She bought me shoeshine to go to the park and clean shoes. My classmates were envious of me and they stopped me and started beating me one day. Mama was passing by the park coming from cleaning the church and saw what was happening. She ran to defend me. We had no shoes and we did whatever we could to survive. God gave us strength and lifted us up because of my mother's prayers. And today we thank God for the life of a great woman who was my mother. I love you mom.

## Testimony of her daughter-in-law Carmen Martínez

I remember when I first arrived in the United States a short time ago, I was at home with my 3-year-old son and I was very sad. That morning I woke up with the memory of my mother who had passed away two years before. I spent the whole day crying. That afternoon Mama Norma came home from work and noticed I was crying and asked me what was wrong. I couldn't hold back the tears and started crying again. Mama said to me "But daughter, why are you like this? Why are you crying?" and I answered, "It's because I feel alone, as if I have no one." She picked me up off my chair and said, "Look, daughter, I never want to hear you say those words again in your life because you are not alone. First, you have God and then you have me. I am your mother, I am the mother that God has given you and I fight for you. I love you like a daughter, so don't ever say that again." And there she hugged me tightly. I could sincerely feel in that hug the pure love and affection she felt for me. From that moment on we became closer and had a very special bond. We were like mother and daughter, daughter and mother. That is how I still remember her as a mother to me.

## Testimony of María Arias

In the summer of 1999, we had a crisis with my son Jorge. I hardly slept and one afternoon I went to bed to rest and I dreamt that I was walking through the streets looking for Jorge. As I was walking, I met a lady who told me "Come, little daughter, look at your son giving testimony of what Jesus did in his life." Then months later we went to Centro Cristiano Adonai church for the first time. There I was surprised to see Mama Norma because I realized that she was the lady I saw in my dreams with my son Jorge.

## Testimony of Brunnell Velázquez

One Sunday morning, Pastor Liliana was preaching and gave a word of knowledge about a woman who had an abortion.

My sister responded to the call and went forward. The pastor put her hand on her belly and began to rebuke the spirit of murder in her. My sister immediately began to manifest and fell to the floor. When she finally stood up, Mama Norma came to her and took her in her arms. She hugged her tightly. And I know that God used Mama Norma's life to minister the Father's love to my sister and to bring inner healing. After that day, my sister was not only free, but she was healed of the deep guilt she carried for her abortion.

## Testimony of Esperanza Araque Machado

All my love and gratitude to Jehovah our God for Mama Norma. I could always feel God's presence in her. Her peace, joy and great wisdom were truly inspiring. Several times I told her that, if I ever reached her age I wanted to be like her. She would hug me and we would laugh so much. She taught me with her infinite love to submit to my husband. I didn't love him at all. And she insisted and insisted.... Do you want to be like me? Do you want to please God? Surrender, submit to your husband. He is the head of the family. I thank Mama Norma for her great teachings. And for her infinite love. Jehovah our God dwelt in her. Although after a while we no longer attended the same church, she never stopped being my friend, my sister, my Mama Norma. She will always be in my heart and thoughts. I am eternally grateful to God for her and her family.

## Testimony of her granddaughter, Yinnet Esther De la Cruz

Mama was the first person who believed in my visions and dreams. I remember when I was 7 years old I used to get up at night and go to the kitchen and stay there for a while. Mama noticed that every night I would get up and go to the kitchen. On the third day she asked me why I was doing that. I told her that I saw a golden ladder and I couldn't see how far it could go. I told her that I saw angels dressed in white with wings of gold, and I could only see a bright light at the top of the stairs. That's when Mom told me that God gave me the gift of seeing visions and having dreams. I replied that the angels were smiling at me and that they knew I was there and I felt so peaceful. She told me at that moment that it meant God had great promises for my life, just as God revealed to Jacob. She told me from that moment on to always tell her about my dreams and visions. Mama always believed in what I saw, she never doubted the things I told her I saw. What she did was pray more for me, that God would continue to reveal himself in my dreams and give me more visions.

I thank God for having had such a faith-based woman who could see and understand beyond the natural, into the supernatural. She was attentive, kind, a very good counselor, she surrounded me with love. She was the rock of my family and my life. She always had a word of faith and hope and thanks to those teachings I am who I am today. I hope I can be half the person she was here on earth. Mama I love you, today, tomorrow and always. I miss you.

## Testimony of Margarita Urbaez (long-time family friend)

I want to tell you part of my testimony of who Sister Norma Martinez was in my life. In 1984, Fernando and Hilcia Carrion, whom I already knew, invited me to JFK airport to meet a very special person, Sister Norma. When she greeted me, she asked me, "So, who are you?" I told her who I was, and she said, "well from now on consider me your mother."

And, from then on, I called her Mama Norma and from that moment on everyone called her Mama Norma. A well-deserved name because she was the mother of multitudes. She was love, understanding and a person who inspired trust.

I remember being very young when I felt afraid or scared of something, I would run to her arms and she knew how to overcome my fear with her love, tenderness and wise words. She was a grandmother to my children and very respected by my husband Pedro. The last time we saw each other, was in the state of Florida without imagining that it would be the last time I would see her. I remember when I was saying goodbye, she called Maria Muniz, her blood daughter and asked her to look for her mantle. A special one she had brought from Israel. Maria said "Mom, it's packed in the luggage already" since they had plans to travel to NY. She said, "well give me another one I want to pray for my daughter Margarita." It was an honor for me to receive her blessing before her departure to meet with our Heavenly Father. It was also very painful for me not to attend her funeral, as I was in delicate health and in the process of a very delicate operation. Thank you, Lord for Mama Norma. It was an honor to have known her. You will always live in my heart. Farewell, I love you.

### Testimony of her grandson, Jhonatan Martínez

I lived with my grandmother until I was 11 or 12 years old. I have many vivid memories of my Abuelita. Every morning before I left for school and on weekends, she demanded that my brother, sister and I hold hands to pray. We could not leave the house before she covered us with the blood of Christ. I remember her putting her dentures away every night before bedtime. One of the memories I have of my Abuelita that I cherish and hold close to my heart was the day she met my daughter, her great-granddaughter, Genesis. She held her in her arms and told me how beautiful my daughter was. I have a picture and video of that great day. I thank God I have it. I can remember the countless times we played "checkers". She taught me how to play when I was about 7 or so. Playing was our thing; we played checkers day and night, night and day. She will always be my partner in it. I miss you very much and I love you grandma, until we play again Mama.

## Testimony of her grandson, Cristóbal Martínez

My grandmother was a woman of great faith. One of the greatest testaments and legacies she left was to teach us all what faith really was. Really, I think she took great joy in showing her grandchildren what it meant to have faith. For me, ever since I was a little kid, I have always seen her as a great woman, a real role model! I always saw a person of great wisdom in her. She knew exactly what to say when a word was needed. Even as an adult, that image of her remains. I can remember how I would tell her when I needed a prayer or was working on something, "Mama, I need you to pray for me. I need this to happen or to work in my favor." She would answer, "Why don't *you* pray and ask for it?" I said, "You have God's direct number; he listens to you more than he listens to me. I will pray about it, but if you pray too, I know he will hear you. It seems like every time I ask you to pray, he comes."

She called me Samuel. One of my best memories was when I was a little boy. One day I was in the living room watching TV and suddenly I heard someone calling me. I ran to her and asked, "Mama, did you call me?" She said no. I went back to watching TV. Once again, I'm there watching TV and I heard someone calling me. And again, I ran to her and said, did you just call me? She again tells me no. I went back one more time and for the third time I heard someone calling me. When I came back to her, I said Mama, are you messing with me? I just heard you call me again. Then she looks at me and says, come sit with me. Then she started telling me about Samuel in the Bible and we started reading about him together. At that moment, she understood that God had a special calling for me. From that day on she always called me Samuel. I remember she gave me the task of reading the two books of Samuel and learning who he was. Every time she saw me she would say "Oh my Samuel" with her sweet and tender voice. It is a part of her that I carry with me every day of my life. When I look back now it all makes so much sense.

I came to the United States at the age of 3 and she lived with us. Right from the beginning, she would take me to church even though my mom and dad weren't yet walking in faith or attending church. She never left me behind. She took it upon herself to dedicate me to God just as Hannah did with Samuel. It is a memory that brings tears to my eyes because it shows me how much love my grandmother had for me.

## Testimony of Nelson Moran

Almost 8 years ago I met Mama Norma, as we all knew her. I saw her every Sunday and there was not a Sunday when she didn't call me son to affirm me and pray for me as if I were her own son or grandson. Those words have never been faded from my heart, mind and feelings because all of those words have helped me see where I am going. For me, Mama Norma is not gone; she has remained in my heart. Mama Norma will always be in me for as she used to tell me that I would be very blessed one day. She always spoke those words to me. She saw in me what I didn't see in myself at that time. Forever Mama

Norma will be in my heart. One day I will prove that the words she prophesied about my life have come true.

## Testimony of Pastors Matt & Diana (Didi) Matthews and The Tribe (King Jesus Int. Ministries)

Norma Martinez would light up any room with her presence. You could walk into a crowded room, feel suffocated or out of place and suddenly, you would see a beautiful, docile smile, with tender, loving eyes looking right at you, and a feeling of peace would come after, in case you weren't so sure if you should be there or not. This would also happen, when we would walk up the aisle, just before preaching. Mama Norma, not only prayed for us, but she was there, front and center to receive and help us preach with all her heart. She was a mother to us! Her love and acceptance for us, and not only for us, but for our children as well, was a game changer for us during our time in New York. We were genuinely amazed that even though she was older and wiser than us, she was always yielding, submitting and taking responsibility for her actions.

What a conqueror she was! I remember one day driving to Valley Stream, New York and going to the same building where I believe the whole family lived. It was a pleasure to be around the whole family; she always instilled peace and gave us the feeling of family warmth that we missed, being away from our loved ones. By the way, she was an amazing cook! I don't know if it was the sancocho soup she once made for us or ajiaco, as we Colombians call it, but the soup she made for us was A BOMB OF DELIGHTS!

This is just a glimpse of how this woman of God had such a powerful and lasting impact on our lives. When she stopped coming to services due to her illness, Hilcia always made sure to give us her greetings; she always made sure to tell us that she was praying for us, and we made sure to send our blessing and love back. When we realized her time to go was approaching, we all made sure to go to her and thank her for so much love; and even though we were there to pray for her and show the family our support, she sat strong and firm in her bed, and prayed fiercely for us. God sent her, no doubt, because she declared a much-needed Word of blessing upon our lives. She reminded us that our work had not been in vain, and that our career was not over: she was unleashing virtue and life upon us, and that impartation we still carry with us today.

Mama Norma will always be a part of our lives. We carry her in our hearts. Her smile, eyes, hugs. We love her very much. We love her still. Until we see her again in heaven, always with love.

## Testimony of her granddaughter, Zoraida López

I thank God for the grandmother that God allowed me to have; a grandmother with a lot of wisdom, patience, love and above all full of the Holy Spirit. My grandmother influenced my life in so many ways that it is difficult to explain in writing. Ever since I was a little girl, God gave me the gift of seeing things through dreams and visions and I would always run to my grandmother to tell her about the visions or dreams that God had given me. She was the one who always interpreted them for me and taught me that no matter what happens, our eyes and trust must always be placed in God and that the altar is sacred. She taught me that family is very important and that, as a family, even though she was going to heaven we had to remain united. When she left for heaven she left a big void in my heart, but what makes me happy is that she is next to her beloved Jesus and I hope that someday, in God's time, we will meet again.

## Testimony of Amanda Carrion

I was all dressed up to go dancing with Abuelita's grandson, Jose Carrion. We were at his parent's house waiting for his friend to pick us up, when each family member slowly started showing up. I had not met any of them yet and wasn't planning to that night. I wouldn't have dreamt that I would meet them in my club clothes! I felt shy and embarrassed. When Abuelita saw me, she gave me the biggest smile with sparkling eyes and opened her arms to embrace me. I knew exactly what she felt and what she felt for me. Unconditional LOVE. At that moment, all of my anxiety and insecurities vanished. They just melted away. I looked around and the rest of the family resembled that love, too. One by one they hugged me without judgment. All genuinely happy to meet me.

I remember the first Thanksgiving at the Carrion family's house in Corona, Queens. Abuelita brought me into the kitchen to help her and Hilcia make pastelitos. She had a fork in her hand and pressed the edges of the dough that wrapped the ground beef; demonstrating what she wanted me to do. Then she handed me a fork and I joined in. Abuelita had a way of making everyone feel wanted, welcome and a part of something big.

Years later, Abuelita, Hilcia, Ruth and Sophia came to our house to be there for the birth of our son, Jude Carrion. I was 41 weeks pregnant and wasn't showing any signs of labor. We would go on walks together to help induce labor. She would hold my hand, smiling and taking in her surroundings. Abuelita had a glow about her that reminded me of classical paintings of people with golden hallows around their heads. I ended up having a planned c-section and a hard recovery. When Jose and I brought Jude home, the house was decorated, and a huge pot of chicken soup AKA Sancocho was waiting for us. It was such a special time for us, and we were grateful to have their support. Abuelita showed me that the love I had longed for exists. She is not gone. She is radiating in heaven.

# Memories of yesterday.
## Photographs of the beautiful life of Norma Martinez.

# Small beginnings:

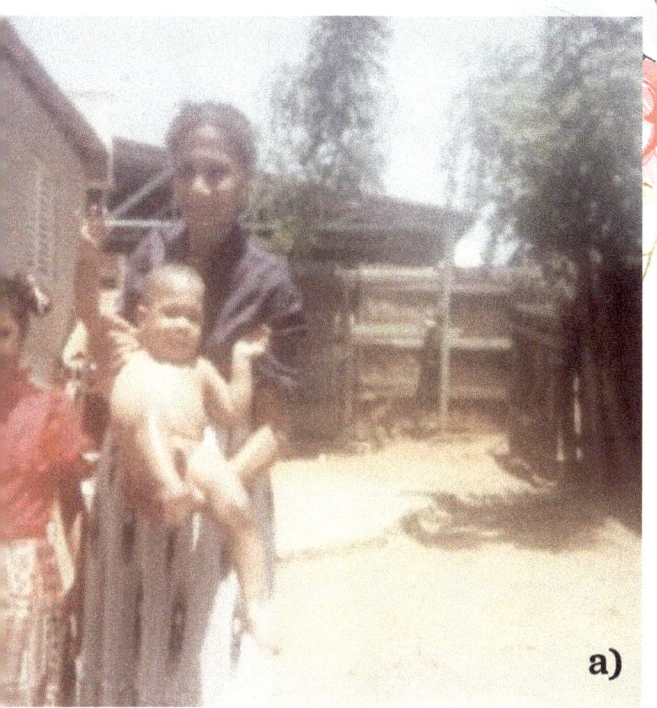

a)

b)

c)

Norma with her daughter Maria and grandson Jose (Dominican Republic, 1979)

Norma with her mother (Dominican Republic, 1975)

Norma with her mother Francisca, son David and daughter María
(Dominican Republic, 1985)

a) Norma with her son in law Fernando and first grandson Jose (Queens, NY 1985)

b) Norma on her 65th birthday (Queens, NY 1997)

c) Norma with the elder she cared for and granddaughter Noemi (Queens, NY 1985)

d) At home with her grandson Jose (Queens, NY 1985)

- Hilcia and Fernando as newlyweds (Santo Domingo, Dominican Republic, 1975)
- Her first experience with snow (Queens, NY 1985)
- Norma and her daugther Hilcia enjoying the Botanical Gardens (Queens, NY 1985)
- Enjoying the snow with her grandson Jose (Queens, NY 1985)

# Ministry

a)

b)

c)

a) With her daughter Hilcia and sisters in the faith (Lirios de los Valles, Queens NY 1987)
b) With Pastor Ezequiel Rosario in Adonai Christian Center (Queens, NY 2003)
c) Preaching in her church Lirios de los Valles (Queens, NY 1986)

a) Preaching and feeding the needy in Dominican Republic during a missons trip (1998)

b) With Pastor Almonte in their church Lirio de los Valles (Queens, NY 1994)

a) Enjoying the children during a missions trip in the Dominican Republic (1998)
b) With Pastors Almonte and José Pentón (Queens, NY 1996)
c) With the children of Bayaguana, Dominican Republic and brother in the faith, Bolívar

a) Preaching and feeding the children.

b) Demonstrating the love of God.

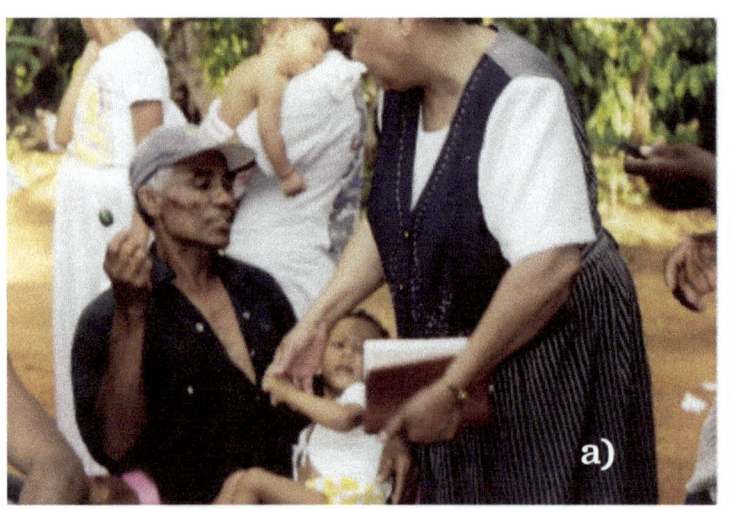

a) Praying for the sick.

b) Bayaguana, Dominican Republic (2003)

a) Trip to Israel with Pastor Rosemary and brothers/sisters in the faith.
b) Missonary trip with José Pentón, Elizabeth Carlo and Flor Tuero (2003)

# Family

a) With her daughter María Muñiz and family (Queens, NY 2007)

b) Norma with her daughter Maribel and family (Queens NY, 2007)

c) Norma with her daughter in law Carmen Martínez and grandchildren (Queens, NY 2007)

d) With her grandchildren celebrating Christmas Eve 'Nochebuena' (Queens, NY 2002)

e) Norma celebrating her birthday surrounded by her favorite kind of flowers (Queens, NY 2008)

With her daughter Rut and granddaughter Ruth during Christmas Eve (Queens, NY 2002)

With her son Cristobal and daughter Rut during her 75th birthday party (Queens, NY 2007)

Praying for her children Cristobal and Jose during a family party (Queens, NY 2003)

With her son in law, Pastor Luciano Muñiz (Queens NY 2005)

With her 8 children celebrating her 75th birthday (Queens, NY 2007)

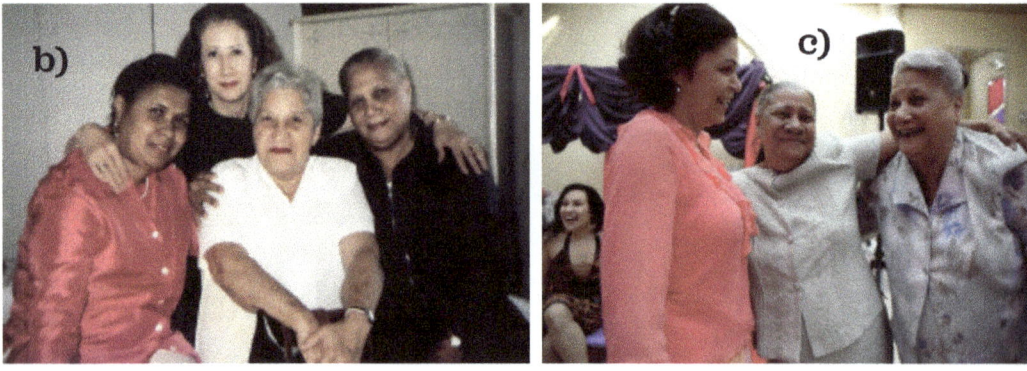

a) With her 8 children and 20 grandchildren during her 75th birthday party (Queens, NY 2007)

b) With her daughter Hilcia, friend Mayela Guidel and Pastor Frank Almonte's moth (Dominican Republic)

c) With her sister Rosa and Pastor Rosemary Almonte during her granddaughter Ruth's bridal shower (Queens, NY 2009)

a) Christmas with some of her grandchildren (Queens, NY 2012)

b) Christmas with her children (Queens, NY 2012)

c) Christmas with some of her grandchildren and great grandchildren
(Queens, NY 2014)

a) Enjoying nature (April 2016)
b) Always enjoying rocking chairs (FL, 2016)
c) Norma with her daughter Hilcia and family (Long Island, NY 2016)

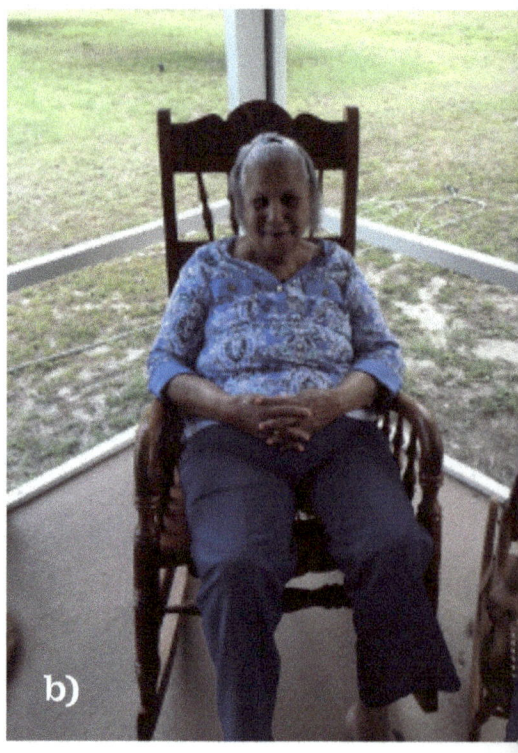

- With her daughters Hilcia and Maria (Miami, FL 2017)
- With her daughter Rut during Thanksgiving (Queens, NY 2016)
- With her sons Juan Feliz, Jose David, Jacinto (stepson), Cristobal, and Jose Daniel for Mother's Day (May 2018)

a)

b)

c)

a)  With her daughters Maria, Maribel, Hilcia and Rut (Mother's Day - Queens, NY May 2018)
b)  Norma with Hilcia and Fernando (Miami FL, 2018)
c)  Saying goodbye to her family before returning to NY (Miami, FL December 2018)
d)  With daughters Maribel and Maria before returning to NY for the last time (Miami, FL 2018)

A very special day receiving her American Citizenship with her son in law Fernando and daughter Hilcia (Miami, FL June 2018)

a)

b)

With her daughters Rut and Maribel, grandchildren and great grandchildren in NY (December 2018)

With her beautiful sister Rosa, together until the very last moments (Queens, NY December 2018)

Norma Martínez's home in Hatomayor del Rey, Dominican Republic
(2018)

# Family Tree

Norma Martínez

**Hilcia Carrion:**

Spouse: Fernando Carrión

Children:

*José Carrion*

Spouse: Amanda Carrion

Son: Jude Carrion

*Noemí Martínez*

Spouse: Luis Martínez

Children: Esther Martínez, Daniel Martínez

*Ruth Arias*

Spouse: Freddy Arias

Children: Sophia Arias, Stephen Arias

*Betania Maldonado*

Spouse: Aarón Maldonado


**José David Martínez:**

Spouse: Belky Martínez

Children:

*José David Martínez Jr.*

*Mother: Altagracia*

Spouse: Iris Nieves Martínez

Children: Ezequias Martínez, Dahirynes Martínez, Abigail Martínez

*Ruth Noemí Martínez* (Mother: Altagracia)

Children: Carlos José Upia, Kelly Bowman

*Joel Martínez* (Mother: Belky)


**José Daniel Mercedes:**

Spouse: Maria Mercedes

Children:

*Yeny Martínez Tejada*

Spouse: Eladio Antonio Duran

Children: Rainel Enmanuel Susana Martínez

*Ruth Noemi Mercedes*

Children: Ruth Ramírez, Orianny Ramírez

*Marlene Martínez*

Children: Darieli Silvestre, Darileyda Silvestre, Daricha Silvestre

*Franklin Mercedes*

*Emmanuel Espaillat*

*Carmen Teresa Lara*

*Atanael Lara*


**Maria Martínez:**

Children:

*Zoraida Esther López*

Spouse: Yunior Manuel López

Children: Rebecca Esther López, Nathan Tahj López

*Claribel Martínez St. Victor*

Spouse: Carlo St. Victor

Son: Jacob Levi St. Victor

*Elías Candelario*

### Juan Félix Martínez:

*Children:*

*Yaritza Martínez*

Son: *Lennox Martínez*

*Rosanna Martínez*

### Ruth Pizarro:

Spouse: Raúl Pizarro

Sons: *Ezequiel Pizarro, Eliezer Pizarro*

### Cristóbal Martínez:

Spouse: María del Carmen Martínez

Children:

*Cristóbal Alexander Martínez*

Spouse: Gloribel Abreu De Martínez

Daughter: Luna Marie Martínez Abreu

*Estephania De la Rosa*

Children: Elian Santana, Liam Santana

*Jhonatan Martínez*

Daughter: Génesis Lee Martínez

*Christopher Kevin De la Cruz*

Spouse: Faendy Garcia Santos

Children: Emiliana De la Cruz, Aizen De la Cruz

*Yinnet Esther De la Cruz*

Spouse: Kelvin De la Cruz

Son: Kayden Adriel De la Cruz

*Christbel Martínez*

## María Muñiz:

Spouse: Luciano Muñiz

Sons: *Joshua Muñiz, Ishmael Muñiz, Samuel Muñiz*

## Stepsons:

Jacinto Martínez

Luis Martínez

José Mercedes

April 1932 - January 2019

# Mama Norma
# Virtuous Woman
## The Wife of Noble Character

[10]A wife of noble character who can find?
She is worth far more than rubies.
[11]Her husband has full confidence in her
and lacks nothing of value.
[12]She brings him good, not harm,
all the days of her life.
[13]She selects wool and flax
and works with eager hands.
[14]She is like the merchant ships,
bringing her food from afar.
[15]She gets up while it is still night;
she provides food for her family
and portions for her female servants.
[16]She considers a field and buys it;
out of her earnings she plants a vineyard.
[17]She sets about her work vigorously;
her arms are strong for her tasks.
[18]She sees that her trading is profitable,
and her lamp does not go out at night.
[19]In her hand she holds the distaff
and grasps the spindle with her fingers.
[20]She opens her arms to the poor
and extends her hands to the needy.
[21]When it snows, she has no fear for her household;
for all of them are clothed in scarlet.
[22]She makes coverings for her bed;
she is clothed in fine linen and purple.

[23]Her husband is respected at the city gate,
where he takes his seat among the eldersof the land.
[24]She makes linen garments and sells them,
and supplies the merchants with sashes.
[25]She is clothed with strength and dignity;
she can laugh at the days to come.
[26]She speaks with wisdom,
and faithful instruction is on her tongue.
[27]She watches over the affairs of her household
and does not eat the bread of idleness.
[28]Her children arise and call her blessed;
her husband also, and he praises her:
[29]"Many women do noble things,
but you surpass them all."
[30]Charm is deceptive, and beauty is fleeting;
but a woman who fears theLORDis to be praised.
[31]Honor her for all that her hands have done,
and let her works bring her praiseat the city gate.

Proverbs 31: 10-31 NIV